A Note From Rick Renner

I am on a personal quest to see a "revival of the Bible" so people can establish their lives on a firm foundation that will stand strong and endure the test when the end-time storm winds begin to intensify.

In order to experience a revival of the Bible in your personal life, it is important to take time each day to read, receive, and apply its truths to your life. James tells us that if we will continue in the perfect law of liberty — refusing to be forgetful hearers but determined to be doers — we will be blessed in our ways. As you watch or listen to the programs in this series and work through this corresponding study guide, I trust that you will search the Scriptures and allow the Holy Spirit to help you hear something new from God's Word that applies specifically to your life. I encourage you to be a doer of the Word that He reveals to you. Whatever the cost, I assure you — it will be worth it.

> Thy words were found, and I did eat them;
> and thy word was unto me the joy and rejoicing of mine heart:
> for I am called by thy name, O Lord God of hosts.
> — Jeremiah 15:16

Your brother and friend in Jesus Christ,

Rick Renner

Unless otherwise indicated, all scripture quotations are taken from the *King James Version* of the Bible.

Scripture quotations marked (*MSG*) are taken from *The Message*, copyright © 1993, 2002, 2018 by Eugene H. Peterson. Used by permission of NavPress. All rights reserved. Represented by Tyndale House Publishers, Inc.

Scripture quotations marked (*TLB*) are taken from *The Living Bible* copyright © 1971. Used by permission of Tyndale House Publishers, Inc., Carol Stream, Illinois 60188. All rights reserved.

Christ's Message to Laodicea

Copyright © 2020 by Rick Renner
8316 E. 73rd St.
Tulsa, Oklahoma 74133

Published by Rick Renner Ministries
www.renner.org

ISBN 13: 978-1-68031-674-2

eBook ISBN 13: 978-1-68031-679-7

All rights reserved. No portion of this book may be reproduced or transmitted in any form or by any means — electronic, mechanical, photocopy, recording, scanning, or other — except for brief quotations in critical reviews or articles, without the prior written permission of the Publisher.

How To Use This Study Guide

This ten-lesson study guide corresponds to *"Christ's Message to Laodicea"* *With Rick Renner* (**Renner TV**). Each lesson in this study guide covers a topic that is addressed during the program series, with questions and references supplied to draw you deeper into your own private study of the Scriptures on this subject.

To derive the most benefit from this study guide, consider the following:

First, watch or listen to the program prior to working through the corresponding lesson in this guide. (Programs can also be viewed at **renner.org** by clicking on the Media/Archives links.)

Second, take the time to look up the scriptures included in each lesson. Prayerfully consider their application to your own life.

Third, use a journal or notebook to make note of your answers to each lesson's Study Questions and Practical Application challenges.

Fourth, invest specific time in prayer and in the Word of God to consult with the Holy Spirit. Write down the scriptures or insights He reveals to you about being filled with the Spirit and empowered by Him in your daily life.

Finally, take action! Whatever the Lord tells you to do according to His Word, do it.

For added insights on this subject, it is recommended that you obtain Rick Renner's books *A Light in Darkness* and *No Room for Compromise*. You may also select from Rick's other available resources by placing your order at **renner.org** or by calling 1-800-742-5593.

TOPIC
History of Laodicea

SCRIPTURES

1. **Revelation 3:14-22** — And unto the angel of the church of the Laodiceans write; These things saith the Amen, the faithful and true witness, the beginning of the creation of God; I know thy works, that thou art neither cold nor hot: I would thou wert cold or hot. So then because thou art lukewarm, and neither cold nor hot, I will spue thee out of my mouth. Because thou sayest, I am rich, and increased with goods, and have need of nothing; and knowest not that thou art wretched, and miserable, and poor, and blind, and naked: I counsel thee to buy of me gold tried in the fire, that thou mayest be rich; and white raiment, that thou mayest be clothed, and that the shame of thy nakedness do not appear; and anoint thine eyes with eyesalve, that thou mayest see. As many as I love, I rebuke and chasten: be zealous therefore, and repent. Behold, I stand at the door, and knock: if any man hear my voice, and open the door, I will come in to him, and will sup with him, and he with me. To him that overcometh will I grant to sit with me in my throne, even as I also overcame, and am set down with my Father in his throne. He that hath an ear, let him hear what the Spirit saith unto the churches.

GREEK WORDS

1. "angel" — ἄγγελος (*angelos*): a human messenger or angel; one sent on a special mission; one dispatched to perform a specific assignment; a delegate or dignitary; pictures the role of a pastor; a messenger of God

2. "church" — ἐκκλησία (*ekklesia*): a called, separated assembly; a prestigious assembly of distinguished citizens who determined laws, debated public policy, formulated new policies, argued and ruled in judicial matters, elected chief magistrates, and decided who should be banished; a body of believers who have been called out, called forth, selected, and assembled to be God's representatives in every town, city, state, or nation; a body called to make decisions that affect the atmosphere of a region

3. "the Amen" — ὁ Ἀμήν (*ho Amen*): definite article with Ἀμήν (*Amen*); literally THE Amen; the word Ἀμήν (*Amen*) describes something faithful, firm, sure, most assuredly, emphatic, or final; can mean "let it be"; the final word; verily

4. "witness" — ὁ μάρτυς (*ho martus*): definite article ὁ (*ho*) with μάρτυς (*martus*); literally, THE Faithful One; however, the word μάρτυς (*martus*) describes one who is summoned to testify in a court of law; legal witnesses were only allowed to speak what was personally known to be true; μάρτυς (*martus*) is connected to the idea of suffering because if one was called to be a witness, he was required to be faithful to the truth, regardless of possible retribution that might be carried out against him by those who opposed his witness or wished to suppress the truth; thus, to be a witness required the highest level of integrity and commitment, as well as a willingness to sacrifice oneself or one's status to uphold the truth

5. "faithful" — ὁ πιστὸς (*ho pistos*): definite article ὁ (*ho*) with πιστὸς (*pistos*); literally, THE Faithful One; faithful, reliable; full of faith; one who kept his faith; one who is worthy of trust; one who can be relied upon

6. "true" — ὁ ἀληθινός (*ho alethinos*): definite article ὁ (*ho*) with ἀληθινός (*alethinos*); literally, THE True One; true, real, bona fide, genuine, indisputable, or authentic

7. "beginning" — ἡ ἀρχὴ (*he arche*): absolutely; of the beginning of all things; the first; denotes principality, rule, magistracy; used also to denote kings and rulers; the very beginning; the initial starting point; what comes first and is hence chief above all; highest in priority; preeminent

8. "creation" — κτίσις (*ktisis*): creation; that which is created out of nothing; the act of creating; refers to the creation of all things

SYNOPSIS

The ten lessons in this study on *Christ's Message to Laodicea* will focus on the following topics:

- The History of Laodicea
- Cold, Hot, or Lukewarm
- Materially Rich

- Spiritually Poor
- Christ's Counsel to the Calloused
- Christ's Rebuke and Chastening of His Church
- Christ Pounding at the Door of the Church
- A Promise of Instant Intimacy for Those Who Open the Door
- The Commitment To Constantly Be Overcoming
- What the Spirit Is Saying to the Church Today

The emphasis of this lesson:

Laodicea was an extremely rich church located between the city of Colossae to the southeast and the city of Hierapolis to the north. It was the last of the seven churches Christ called to account in His visitation to John on the isle of Patmos.

What Do We Know About Laodicea?

Originally, the city of Laodicea was called Diospolis which means the "City of Zeus." Years later, Antiochus II built on top of the ruins of Diospolis and renamed the city Laodicea in honor of his wife Laodice. It was located in the heart of the Lycus Valley between Hierapolis, which was about six miles to the north, and Colossae, approximately nine miles to the southeast. On a good, clear day, you could see the cities of Colossae and Hierapolis from Laodicea.

Hierapolis was a large military city with a church that had been founded by believers from Colossae. It was renowned for its hot mineral water. Colossae was a smaller resort town. It also had a church; however, it was known for its refreshing cold waters. Snow melting atop the mountains to the north naturally flowed down to this city. When the weather was hot and people wanted to be refreshed, they went to Colossae.

Laodicea was the richest city in the region, nestled among many other rich cities. It was filled with fabulous architecture and massive buildings. Although most cities had one theater, Laodicea had two. It also had a huge stadium that could accommodate up to 60,000 people. As far as marketplaces, or *agoras*, Laodicea had four — accommodating more than 4,500 shops. Moreover, it was a banking center and a bustling hub for the textile industry — producing expensive black sheep wool. Of all that

Laodicea was known for, its famous medical school was at the top of the list. It specialized in eye diseases and was well known for its production of "Phrygian powder"—a medicine used for treating eye diseases.

The Message to the Church in Laodicea

Indeed, Laodicea was a city like no other—fabulously rich beyond belief. It was to the believers in this city that Jesus Himself sent this message through the apostle John, saying:

> **And unto the angel of the church of the Laodiceans write; These things saith the Amen, the faithful and true witness, the beginning of the creation of God; I know thy works, that thou art neither cold nor hot: I would thou wert cold or hot. So then because thou art lukewarm, and neither cold nor hot, I will spue thee out of my mouth (Revelation 3:14-16).**

Jesus went on to explain, "Because thou sayest, I am rich, and increased with goods, and have need of nothing; and knowest not that thou art wretched, and miserable, and poor, and blind, and naked: I counsel thee to buy of me gold tried in the fire, that thou mayest be rich; and white raiment, that thou mayest be clothed, and that the shame of thy nakedness do not appear; and anoint thine eyes with eyesalve, that thou mayest see. As many as I love, I rebuke and chasten: be zealous therefore, and repent" (Revelation 3:17-19).

Jesus called on this church to repent and made an amazing promise to those who repented. Jesus said, "Behold, I stand at the door, and knock: if any man hear my voice, and open the door, I will come in to him, and will sup with him, and he with me. To him that overcometh will I grant to sit with me in my throne, even as I also overcame, and am set down with my Father in his throne. He that hath an ear, let him hear what the Spirit saith unto the churches" (Revelation 3:20-22).

Who Was the 'Angel' of the Church in Laodicea?

In Revelation 3:14, Jesus began His message saying, "And unto the angel of the church of the Laodiceans write…." Interestingly, this is the seventh time we see the phrase "the angel of the church." It is the same way Jesus addressed all the churches in the book of Revelation — the church in Ephesus (*see* Revelation 2:1), in Smyrna (*see* Revelation 2:8), in Pergamum (*see* Revelation 2:12), in Thyatira (*see* Revelation 2:18), in

Sardis (*see* Revelation 3:1), in Philadelphia (*see* Revelation 3:7), and lastly in Laodicea.

The word "angel" here is the Greek word *angelos*, and it describes *a human messenger or angel; one sent on a special mission; one dispatched to perform a specific assignment; a delegate or dignitary.* Here it pictures *the role of a pastor acting as a messenger of God.* Thus, the "angel of the church in Laodicea" was the *pastor* of the church.

When Jesus spoke to the believers in Laodicea — as well as to the believers in the other six churches — He first spoke directly to the pastor. This is what He always did. It demonstrated His respect and honor for the line of authority He had established.

Your pastor is a dignitary of Heaven sent as a messenger of God to speak God's heart and to shepherd you. His primary job is to hear what Jesus is saying to the church; he is to understand it, process it, and assimilate it as his own. Then he is to take the message and deliver it to the congregation in the power of the Holy Spirit.

What the Word 'Church' Means

Now that we know the word "angel" — the Greek word *angelos* — refers to the *pastor*, let's examine what the word "church" means. The word "church" is one of the most significant revelations in the entire New Testament. It is the Greek word *ekklesia*, which is a compound of the word *ek*, meaning *out*, and a form of the word *kaleo*, meaning *to call.* When these words are compounded to form *ekklesia*, it describes *a called, separated assembly; a prestigious assembly of distinguished citizens who determined laws, debated public policy, formulated new policies, argued and ruled in judicial matters, elected chief magistrates, and decided who should be banished.*

What's interesting is that the earliest use of the word *ekklesia* was not in connection with the Church at all. It was a secular term first used in the city of Athens to describe the prestigious, political body of citizens who were summoned from society to rule in the decisions of public policy and government. This group of 6,000 individuals met regularly on a hill near the Acropolis and was led by the *kerux*, which is the New Testament word for a "preacher." The *kerux* gave the *ekklesia* principles, facts, and information they needed in order to vote and rule effectively.

The writers of the New Testament understood the meaning of the word *ekklesia*. By selecting this word, the Holy Spirit is letting us know that we — the Church — are *a body of believers who have been called out, called forth, selected, and assembled to be God's representatives in every town, city, state, or nation*. We are not just a group of insignificant nobodies who meet in various buildings or random places. We are a body called out to make decisions that affect the atmosphere of a region.

Jesus Described Himself As…
THE AMEN

Once Jesus instructed John to write to the angel of the church in Laodicea, He then described Himself in a very unique way, placing Himself in a category all His own. He said, "…These things saith the Amen, the faithful and true witness, the beginning of the creation of God" (Revelation 3:14).

In each of these titles, there is a definite article attached, which is what elevates Jesus into a category all His own. The definite article is the Greek word *ho*, translated as the word "the." Hence, Jesus is not *an* Amen — He is THE Amen! The word "amen" describes *something faithful, firm, and sure*. It means *most assuredly, emphatic, or final*. It can also mean *let it be; the final word*; or *verily*.

THE FAITHFUL AND TRUE WITNESS

Next Jesus describes Himself as "the Faithful and True Witness." The word "witness" is the Greek word *martus*, and it is where we get the word "martyr." It describes *one who is summoned to testify in a court of law*. In early New Testament times, legal witnesses were only allowed to speak what was personally known to be true. Hence, a "witness" (*martus*) is connected to the idea of suffering, because if one was called to be a witness, he was required to be faithful to the truth regardless of possible retribution that might be carried against him by those who opposed his witness or wished to suppress the truth. Thus, to be a witness required the highest level of integrity and commitment, as well as a willingness to sacrifice oneself or one's status to uphold the truth.

Again we see that the definite article *ho* — translated as "the" — precedes the word *martus*. As such, these words should be translated "*the* Faithful and True Witness." In other words, Jesus is not just *a* witness; He is THE

Witness. No one has more integrity and commitment than Him! He is *the* ultimate example of bravery in hard times who stood by the truth regardless of the price He had to pay.

The Bible also says Jesus is "faithful," which in Greek is the word *pistos*, meaning *faithful, reliable; full of faith; one who kept his faith; one who is worthy of trust; one who can be relied upon.* Again, the definite article *ho* — translated as "the" — precedes the word *pistos.* Hence, Jesus is literally declaring Himself to be "*the* Faithful One" or "*the* Trustworthy One." There is no one more faithful and reliable and worthy of trust than Him.

Furthermore, Jesus is also identified as "true." The word "true" is the Greek word *alethinos*, which means *true, real, bona fide, genuine, indisputable, or authentic.* It, too, has the definite article *ho* attached to it — *ho alethinos.* Thus, it literally means Jesus is not just *a* Truth; He is THE Truth. He is the *true, real, bona fide, genuine, indisputable, authentic one.*

Putting the meanings of all these words together, here is the *Renner Interpretive Version (RIV)* of this part of Revelation 3:14:

> **These things says He who is THE witness, THE faithful and reliable One who is absolutely trustworthy, THE One who is absolutely true and indisputable....**

THE BEGINNING OF CREATION

Jesus concluded verse 14 by declaring Himself to be "...the beginning of the creation of God." Once again, a definite article precedes the word "beginning." In Greek, "the beginning" is *he arche.* The word *arche* describes *the initial starting point; what comes first and is hence chief above all; highest in priority; preeminent.* Because the definite article is included, it means that Jesus is not *a* beginning — He is absolutely "THE very beginning of all things." He is the Originator of the creation of God.

The word "creation" is the Greek word *ktisis* and denotes *that which is created out of nothing.* It is *the act of creating* and refers to *the creation of all things.* This portion of Scripture lets us know that Jesus was — *and is* — the starting point, the Creator, who created everything we see out of nothing. He is the Truth above all truths, the Supreme Witness, and the Faithful and Trustworthy One. This is the Jesus whom we serve.

In our next lesson, we will examine what Jesus meant when He told the church in Laodicea that they were "neither cold nor hot," but "lukewarm"

— and because they were "lukewarm," He would spue them out of His mouth.

STUDY QUESTIONS

Study to shew thyself approved unto God, a workman that needeth not to be ashamed, rightly dividing the word of truth.
— 2 Timothy 2:15

1. What new facts did you learn about the city of Laodicea in this lesson?

2. As you read through Christ's message to the church in Laodicea in Revelation 3:14-22, what is your first impression of this church? What issues does Jesus seem to have with these believers?

3. One of the ways Jesus identifies Himself in Revelation 3:14 is as "… the beginning of the creation of God." Carefully read John 1:1-3, Colossians 1:15-17, First Corinthians 8:6, and Hebrews 1:1,2, and tell how these passages repeatedly confirm Jesus' declaration.

PRACTICAL APPLICATION

But be ye doers of the word, and not hearers only,
deceiving your own selves.
— James 1:22

1. When you hear that the "angel of the church" is actually the *pastor* of the church, does it help you view your pastor with greater appreciation and respect? What do you see about his role that you didn't see previously?

2. Reread the section on the meaning of the word "church" — the Greek word *ekklesia*. How does this change the way you see the Church's role in society? How does it change the way you see *yourself* as a part of the Church?

TOPIC

Cold, Hot, or Lukewarm

SCRIPTURES

1. **Revelation 3:14-16** — And unto the angel of the church of the Laodiceans write; These things saith the Amen, the faithful and true witness, the beginning of the creation of God; I know thy works, that thou art neither cold nor hot: I would thou wert cold or hot. So then because thou art lukewarm, and neither cold nor hot, I will spue thee out of my mouth.

GREEK WORDS

1. "I know" — οἶδα (*oida*): to see, perceive, understand, or comprehend; pictures knowledge gained by personal experience or personal observation

2. "works" — ἔργα (*erga*): deeds, actions, or activities

3. "that" — ὅτι (*hoti*): specifically; in context, points to what Christ knows about them

4. "cold" — ψυχρός (*psuchros*): not merely cool, but cold; used to depict cold water

5. "hot" — ζεστός (*zestos*): not merely warm, but hot; used to depict boiling hot water

6. "I would" — ὄφελον (*ophelon*): would that; used to express an unattainable wish; it means, "Oh that," "How I wish that," or "I would that"; a deep desire for something that will probably not occur

7. "So then because" — οὕτως ὅτι (*houtos hoti*): the word οὕτως (*houtos*) means "consequently"; the word ὅτι (*hoti*) points to something definitive; "consequently, here is where this is headed"

8. "lukewarm" — χλιαρός (*chliaros*): tepid; lukewarm; indifferent; having lost temperature and it has thereby lost value

9. "spue thee" — σε ἐμέσαι (*se emesai*): the word σε (*se*) is placed first, drawing attention to the hearers; the word ἐμέσαι (*emesai*): is from

ἐμέω (*emeo*), which means to vomit; to throw up; to reject something because its taste is disgusting

10. "out" — ἐκ (*ek*): out; to make an exit

11. "my mouth" — τοῦ στόματός μου (*tou stomatos mou*): the word στόματός (*stomatos*) is mouth; the word μου (*mou*) means "of mine"; together, "of my own mouth"

SYNOPSIS

As we saw in our first lesson, Laodicea was an exceedingly wealthy and affluent city situated in the heart of the Lycus Valley in the Roman province of Asia. As rich as its residents were, their geographic location had left them without a local source of hot water or cold water. Thus, they decided to do something that had not been done by anyone else in history. They created immediate access to both cold and hot running water.

About nine miles southeast of Laodicea was the city of Colossae, and just above Colossae were snow-covered mountains. When the snow melted in spring and summer, refreshing cold water would flow into Colossae. About six miles to the north of Laodicea was the city of Hierapolis, and it was the home to hot mineral springs. Engineers from Laodicea developed a system of pipes to carry cold water from Colossae and hot water from Hierapolis into Laodicea.

With great anticipation, the people waited to receive the refreshing, ice-cold water from the southeast and the medicinal, super-hot water from the north. History reveals that when the system of aqueducts was finally completed and the day came for the Laodiceans to taste the water, the water was putrid and made the people want to vomit. Apparently, the clay pipes could not keep the hot water hot or the cold water cold. Even worse, the mineral elements in the pipes leached out into the water as it traveled to Laodicea, making it extremely distasteful by the time it arrived. All these details are vital to understanding why Jesus said what He said to the church of Laodicea.

The emphasis of this lesson:

The church of Laodicea was birthed by a powerful move of God. But over the years, their fiery love had dwindled, leaving them miserably mediocre and lukewarm. Their influence brought neither healing nor

refreshing to others. Consequently, their fellowship had become putrid to Jesus' taste.

Jesus Is Fully Aware of the Condition of His Church

In Revelation 3:15 and 16, Christ begins to point out the shortcomings of the Laodiceans. He said, "I know thy works, that thou art neither cold nor hot: I would thou wert cold or hot. So then because thou art lukewarm, and neither cold nor hot, I will spue thee out of my mouth."

The words "I know" in verse 14 is the Greek word *oida*, which means *to see, perceive, understand, or comprehend*; it pictures *knowledge gained by personal experience or personal observation*. Jesus' use of this word is the equivalent of Him saying, "There are things about you that I have personally seen with My own eyes. No angel has told Me these things, neither did I learn about them from another person's prayers."

Of what did Jesus have firsthand knowledge? He said, "I know thy works...." The word "works" in Greek is the word *erga*, and it describes *deeds, actions, or activities*. Actually, the Greek structure of this portion of Scripture literally states, "I know by personal observation the deeds, actions, and activities *of you* and *that are unique to you*. There is nothing about you I do not know." The same thing can be said of us today. Jesus knows every single detail about every church and every person in His Church.

Jesus Wants Us To Be 'Cold' or 'Hot'

Specifically, He told the Laodiceans, "I know thy works, that thou art neither cold nor hot: I would thou wert cold or hot" (Revelation 3:15). At first glance, one might logically think that it would be better to be lukewarm — not extreme, but moderate. However, this was not Jesus' view. He would rather them (and *us*) be cold or hot, *not* lukewarm.

The word "cold" is the Greek word *psuchros*, which means *not merely cool, but cold*. It is a word used to depict *freezing-cold water*. The word "hot" in Greek is the word *zestos*, which means *not merely warm, but hot*. This word was used to depict *boiling-hot water*. Essentially, Jesus told the believers in Laodicea, "You're not freezing-cold or boiling-hot. I would that you were freezing cold or boiling hot."

When Jesus said "I would," the apostle John used the word *ophelon*, which means, "I would that." This word was used to express *an unattainable wish*. It was the equivalent of one's saying, "Oh that," "How I wish that," or "I would that." It was an expression communicating *a deep desire for something that will probably not occur*. Jesus deeply desired the Laodicean church to change, but from all that He personally knew about them, He knew it probably would not occur.

Laodicea Was Stuck in the Middle

As we noted in the introduction, Laodicea was located in the middle of two dominant cities — Colossae to the southeast and Hierapolis to the north. Colossae was a resort town that people flocked to during the sweltering heat to enjoy the refreshing, freezing-cold waters from the mountains. Hierapolis, on the other hand, was famous for its hot mineral springs. In fact, it was so legendary that history tells us Cleopatra and Mark Anthony met there to bathe in its healing waters.

When Jesus said to Laodicea, "…I would thou wert cold or hot" (Revelation 3:15), He had these two cities in mind and the resources they were known for. He was aware that engineers had built a remarkable system of aqueducts designed to bring the freezing-cold waters from Colossae and the hot medicinal waters from Hierapolis into Laodicea. He also knew that by the time the waters reached Laodicea, both had become lukewarm.

Not only was the water tepid, but it was also putrid. As it was transported through the clay conduits, it became tainted and developed a horrible taste by the time it reached Laodicea. Thus, the cold water was no longer freezing-cold and refreshing, and the boiling-hot mineral water had lost its heat and healing properties. By Jesus' saying, "I wish that you were cold or hot," He was actually saying, "I wish you had the refreshing properties of the freezing-cold waters of Colossae or the boiling-hot, healing properties of the waters of Hierapolis."

Laodicea Had Lost Its Revitalizing Value

In Revelation 3:16, Jesus went on to say, "So then because thou art lukewarm, and neither cold nor hot, I will spue thee out of my mouth." The phrase "so then because" in Greek is *houtos hoti*. The word *houtos* means "consequently"; the word *hoti* points to *something definitive*. Taken together, the words *houtos hoti* mean, *"Consequently, here is where this is headed."*

This brings us to the word "lukewarm," which is the Greek word *chliaros*. It describes *something tepid, lukewarm*; or *indifferent*. It indicates *something that has lost temperature and it has thereby lost value.* The use of the word *chliaros* — translated here as "lukewarm" — is the equivalent of Jesus' telling the church of Laodicea, "You have lost your value. You are no longer refreshing or providing healing like you once did."

Because they had become indifferent and lost their value, Jesus said, "...I will spue thee out of my mouth." The words "spue thee" in Greek is *se emesai.* The word *se* is placed first, drawing attention to the hearers; the word *emesai* is from the word *emeo*, which means *to vomit; to throw up; to reject something because its taste is disgusting.*

The word "out" is the Greek word *ek*, which means *out* or *to make an exit.* And the phrase "my mouth" is a translation of the Greek phrase *tou stomatos mou.* The word *stomatos* is *mouth*; the word *mou* means *of mine*; together the words mean *"out of my own mouth."* Basically, Jesus said, "Because you are lukewarm and have lost your revitalizing qualities, your fellowship has become disgusting to Me. Therefore, I'm going to vomit you out of My mouth."

Jesus Confronted Laodicea Because He Loved Them

Some may wonder — *did Jesus still love the Laodicean church?* The answer is yes — He most certainly loved them. The truth is, He confronted them *because* He loved them so much. When Jesus is concerned about our spiritual condition, He doesn't mince words. He gets straight to the point and reveals to us what is wrong in our lives.

As we continue our study of *Christ's Message to Laodicea*, we are going to see just how candid He was. In fact, He told them, "You think and say you're rich and don't need anything, but the truth is you're poor, blind, and naked. The church you are now is nowhere near the caliber of church you were when you first began. And while I once enjoyed your life-giving fellowship, it has now become nauseating to My taste."

Just as Jesus had come to expect certain things from the believers in Laodicea, He expects certain things from us. That is, He expects us to be red hot in our love for Him and to bring revitalization and refreshing healing to others. When we become lukewarm — when we have a nonchalant, take-it-or-leave-it attitude about the things of God and God Himself — it is very distasteful to Jesus.

Friend, it is in your best interest to stop and examine yourself. Are you still cold and refreshing to others and to Jesus? Are you still "hot," possessing a medicinal healing quality that those around you desperately need? If you find yourself wanting in one or both of these areas, pray and ask God to light a fresh fire for Him in your heart so you can produce these qualities once again.

STUDY QUESTIONS

> Study to shew thyself approved unto God, a workman that needeth
> not to be ashamed, rightly dividing the word of truth.
> — 2 Timothy 2:15

1. There are passages throughout Scripture that reveal God's expectations of us. What verses come to mind that personally speak to you about what God expects from you?

2. Take time to reflect on these memorable commandments from God's Word. What recurring requirements can you identify in the following passages? Which one(s) do you need God's help with to come up higher in your level of your love for God and others?
   - **Exodus 20:3-17**
   - **Mathew 22:36-40**
   - **Micah 6:8**
   - **Romans 13:9**
   - **James 1:27, 2:8**

PRACTICAL APPLICATION

> But be ye doers of the word, and not hearers only,
> deceiving your own selves.
> — James 1:22

1. Clearly, the church in Laodicea had become lukewarm, and Jesus was disgusted and repulsed by their condition. If Jesus were to appear to you at this very moment, what would He say about *your* condition?

Would He find you to be *boiling hot*, *refreshingly cold*, or *lukewarm* in your relationship with Him?

2. In what areas of your life has your fiery devotion to Him been reduced to a flicker? What practical steps can you take to "fan into flames" your love for Jesus?

3. History reveals that the city of Laodicea attempted to bring the refreshing cold waters of Colossae and the hot medicinal waters of Hierapolis to its people, but they failed. How does their undesirable outcome help you understand what Jesus was saying to the believers in Laodicea about being lukewarm? What does it say to you personally?

LESSON 3

TOPIC

Materially Rich

SCRIPTURES

1. **Revelation 3:14-17** — And unto the angel of the church of the Laodiceans write; These things saith the Amen, the faithful and true witness, the beginning of the creation of God; I know thy works, that thou art neither cold nor hot: I would thou wert cold or hot. So then because thou art lukewarm, and neither cold nor hot, I will spue thee out of my mouth. Because thou sayest, I am rich, and increased with goods, and have need of nothing; and knowest not that thou art wretched, and miserable, and poor, and blind, and naked.

GREEK WORDS

1. "I know" — **οἶδα** (*oida*): to see, perceive, understand, or comprehend; pictures knowledge gained by personal experience or personal observation

2. "works" — **ἔργα** (*erga*): deeds, actions, or activities

3. "that" — **ὅτι** (*hoti*): specifically; in context, points to what Christ knows about them

4. "cold" — **ψυχρός** (*psuchros*): not merely cool, but cold; used to depict cold water

5. "hot" — **ζεστός** (*zestos*): not merely warm, but hot; used to depict boiling hot water

6. "I would" — **ὄφελον** (*ophelon*): would that; used to express an unattainable wish; it means, "Oh that," "How I wish that," or "I would that"; a deep desire for something that will probably not occur

7. "So then because" — **οὕτως ὅτι** (*houtos hoti*): the word **οὕτως** (*houtos*) means "consequently"; the word **ὅτι** (*hoti*) points to something definitive; "consequently, here is where this is headed"

8. "lukewarm" — **χλιαρός** (*chliaros*): tepid; lukewarm; indifferent; having lost temperature and it has thereby lost value

9. "spue thee" — **σε ἐμέσαι** (*se emesai*): the word **σε** (*se*) is placed first, drawing attention to the hearers; the word **ἐμέσαι** (*emesai*): is from **ἐμέω** (*emeo*), which means to vomit; to throw up; to reject something because its taste is disgusting

10. "out" — **ἐκ** (*ek*): out; to make an exit

11. "my mouth" — **τοῦ στόματός μου** (*tou stomatos mou*): the word **στόματός** (*stomatos*) is mouth; the word **μου** (*mou*) means "of mine"; together, "out of my own mouth"

12. "because" — **ὅτι** (*hoti*): specifically; in context, points to what Christ has concluded about them

13. "thou sayest" — **λέγεις** (*legeis*): you allege; you say; not necessarily based on fact, but expresses their flawed opinion of themselves

14. "I am" — **εἰμι** (*eimi*): I am; points to self-reliance, self-focus, self-centeredness, even self-absorption; indicates they are the center of their world

15. "rich" — **Πλούσιός** (*Plousios*): wealth so great it cannot be tabulated; abundant or vast wealth; extreme riches; unlimited wealth; incredible abundance; opulence; extravagant lavishness; someone who possesses incredible abundance, extreme wealth, and enormous affluence; magnificent wealth; here it is capitalized, possibly meaning "the Richest"

16. "increased with goods" — **πεπλούτηκα** (*peploutika*): from **πλουτέω** (*plouteo*), rich, endowed with resources; in this text, I have made myself rich; I have resourced myself

17. "need of nothing" — οὐδὲν χρείαν (*ouden chreian*): the word οὐδὲν (*ouden*) means "absolutely nothing"; the word χρείαν (*chreian*) depicts a need or deficit; absolutely no need of anything whatsoever

18. "have" — ἔχω (*echo*): have; hold; possess

SYNOPSIS

The ancient city of Laodicea was a big, bustling town in the heart of the Lycus Valley. It was the wealthiest among all its neighbors, operating as an epicenter of commerce and trade. This luxurious city had a thriving banking center and textile industry. And apparently the church in Laodicea was wealthy too. When Jesus addressed them in Revelation 3, He recited back to them what they were saying about themselves: "...I am rich, and increased with goods, and have need of nothing..." (Revelation 3:17).

Unfortunately when we are financially well-off, we can become blind to our spiritual need and tend to forget about God. Although Jesus is not against us being blessed, He is against the attitude of pride and indifference toward Him that we can give place to when we experience success and times of plenty. The church in Laodicea is a perfect example of this.

The emphasis of this lesson:

The church of Laodicea was extremely wealthy, just like the city in which it existed. Unfortunately their affluence gave way to pride and blinded them to the fact that it was God who had blessed them with what they had. They were not a self-made success.

Jesus began dictating His message to the church in Laodicea saying, "And unto the angel of the church of the Laodiceans write; These things saith the Amen, the faithful and true witness, the beginning of the creation of God" (Revelation 3:14).

We discovered in our first lesson that Jesus Christ is in a category all His own. He is *the* Amen, which indicates that He has the final word on everything. He is also *the* best Witness of all witnesses — none is better and no one has sacrificed and suffered more to stand by the truth. Moreover, He is *the* Faithful One — the One who can always be relied upon as trustworthy.

Furthermore, Jesus is also "the beginning of the creation of God," which means He is the Originator of all creation — the very One who spoke the world, and everything in it, into existence. His preeminent role is confirmed by the apostle John in John 1:1-3 and by Paul in Colossians 1:15-17.

'I Know Thy Works'

In Revelation 3:15, Jesus spoke bluntly and told the Laodiceans, "I know thy works, that thou art neither cold nor hot: I would thou wert cold or hot." In our last lesson, we saw that the words "I know" is the Greek word *oida*, which means *to see, perceive, understand, or comprehend*. It describes *knowledge gained by personal experience or personal observation*.

We know from Revelation 2:1 that Jesus is in the very center of His Church, walking around and personally observing all that is taking place. That is why He was able to say, "I know (*oida*) thy works" to all seven of the churches in the province of Asia. Jesus' use of the word *oida* is the same as His saying, "There are things about you that I have personally seen with My own eyes. No angel has told Me these things, neither did I learn about them from another person's prayers."

What had Jesus personally seen? He said, "…thy works…." The word "works" in Greek is *erga*, and it describes *deeds, actions, or activities*. A literal translation of the phrase "I know thy works" would be, "I personally know about all your deeds, actions, and activities *that are specific to you*. There is nothing about you I don't know." What was true of Jesus and the Church *then* is true of Him and the Church *now*. He is still walking in the midst of His Church and personally observing and noting the idiosyncrasies of each believer.

'I Would Thou Wert Cold or Hot'

Jesus went on to say, "…thou art neither cold nor hot: I would thou wert cold or hot" (Revelation 3:15). We have seen that the words "cold" and "hot" are references directly linked to water. "Cold" is the Greek word *psuchros*, which is *not merely cool, but cold*; it is used to depict *freezing-cold water*. The word "hot" is the Greek word *zestos*, and it denotes *not merely warm, but hot*; it is used to depict *boiling-hot water*.

Jesus used these words to give the believers in Laodicea an illustration they could easily understand. If you remember, Laodicea was in the middle of two leading cities: Colossae to the southeast and Hierapolis to the north. Colossae was a resort town known for its refreshing cold waters that attracted tourists during hot temperatures, and Hierapolis was famous for its hot springs that brought healing.

When Jesus said, "...I would thou wert cold or hot," the words "I would" is the Greek word *ophelon*, and it was used to express *an unattainable wish*. It was the equivalent of saying, "Oh that...," or "How I wish that...." It is *a deep desire for something that will probably not occur*. Thus, Jesus told the believers in Laodicea, "Oh, how I wish that you were still refreshing like the freezing-cold waters of Colossae or that you were still boiling-hot like the medicinal waters of Hierapolis. Even though it is highly unlikely to happen, I am still hopeful that you will change."

Laodicea Made Jesus Sick to His Stomach

Jesus continued in verse 16 saying, "So then because thou art lukewarm, and neither cold nor hot, I will spue thee out of my mouth." We noted that the phrase "so then because" is *houtos hoti* in Greek. The word *houtos* means *consequently*, and the word *hoti* points to *something definitive*. Hence, *houtos hoti* means *consequently, here is where this is headed*.

The definitive consequence of being neither cold nor hot is being "lukewarm." The Greek word for "lukewarm" is *chliaros*, and it describes *something tepid*, *lukewarm*, or *indifferent*. It signifies *having lost temperature and has thereby lost value*.

The believers in Laodicea were familiar with something that was "lukewarm" and had lost its value. Remember, it was the first city in history to construct massive aqueducts to transport refreshing, cold water and hot, medicinal water from outside sources. Engineers had worked tirelessly to complete the pipelines between their city and the cities of Colossae and Hierapolis. All the while the expectation and anticipation of the residents of Laodicea intensified. But by the time the pipelines had been completed, the cold water from Colossae and the hot water from Hierapolis arrived in Laodicea lukewarm. Both had lost their value. Worse yet, when the people tasted the water from Hierapolis, they vomited it out of their mouths because it tasted disgusting.

Similarly Jesus had great expectations of the church in Laodicea, just as He has great expectations for every church and every believer. Think about it — He invested everything He had to provide for our needs and position us to succeed. He surrendered His body and His life's Blood to bring us

His Holy Spirit and infuse us with God's empowerment so that we might bear eternal fruit and bring Him glory (*see* John 15:16).

When Jesus' expectations for the church in Laodicea were not met, He told them, "…I will spue thee out of my mouth" (Revelation 3:16). The phrase "I will spue thee" in Greek is *se emesai*. The word *se* is placed first, drawing attention to the hearers. This was Jesus' way of telling the Laodiceans, "Hey, I'm talking directly to you." The word *emesai* is from the word *emeo*, which means *to vomit; to throw up; or to reject something because its taste is disgusting*. Jesus said, "I'm going to vomit you Laodiceans right out of My mouth because your fellowship is no longer enjoyable to Me."

Pride Had Blinded Them to the Goodness of God

What was the reason for Laodicea's lukewarm condition? Jesus begins to reveal it in Revelation 3:17, saying, "Because thou sayest, I am rich, and increased with goods, and have need of nothing…." This is quite an amazing statement packed with great meaning.

First, notice the word "because." It is the Greek word *hoti*, which is often translated as the word *that* and points to *something very specific* — something Christ has concluded about them from His personal observation. The words "thou sayest" in Greek is the term *legeis*, which means *you allege; you say*. It is *something not necessarily based on fact*, but expresses the Laodicean's flawed opinion of themselves.

What was this church saying about itself? It was saying, "…I am rich, and increased with goods, and have need of nothing…." The words "I am" in Greek is the word *eimi*, which means *I am* and points to *self-reliance, self-focus, self-centeredness*, and *even self-absorption*. It indicates that the Laodiceans had become *the center of their world*.

The word "rich" is the Greek word *Plousios*, and it describes *wealth so great it cannot be tabulated; abundant or vast wealth; extreme riches; unlimited wealth; incredible abundance; opulence; extravagant lavishness*. This word denotes *someone who possesses incredible abundance, extreme wealth, and enormous affluence*. Although the word *Plousios* always carries the idea of *magnificent wealth*, what is unique about its appearance here is that it is capitalized; possibly meaning *The Richest* of all.

Factually speaking Laodicea was the richest of all the surrounding cities in the Lycus Valley. It had more than 4,500 shops, four huge markets, two theaters, a medical school, a 60,000 seat stadium, a thriving textile industry, and it served as the banking center of the region. Indeed, Laodicea was exceedingly rich, and the carvings in the ruins that are visible today confirm it.

The phrase "increased with goods" is the Greek word *peploutika*, from the word *plouteo*, meaning *rich, endowed with resources*. In the context here, it is the equivalent of saying, "I have made myself rich; I have resourced myself." Herein lies the root of the problem with the church in Laodicea: they were full of pride regarding what they possessed, and they believed they had achieved these things on their own.

Along with this, the Laodicean believers said, "…[we] have need of nothing." The word "have" is the Greek word *echo*, which means *to have, hold, or possess*. And the phrase "need of nothing" is a translation of the Greek words *ouden cheiran*. The word *ouden* means *absolutely nothing*, and the word *cheiran* depicts *a need or deficit*. When these words come together, it means *absolutely no need of anything whatsoever*.

Learn a Lesson from Laodicea

The church of Laodicea is a picture of what happens to a person or a group of people who enters into pride. They became the center of their own world, and their self-centeredness caused them to become independent, self-reliant and forget God. They also forgot about the needs of others as well as their own spiritual need.

Putting the meanings of all these words together, here is the *Renner Interpretive Version (RIV)* of the first part of Revelation 3:17:

> **Because you keep on bragging, I am rich, wealthy, influential, the Richest of all, and I have endowed myself with vast goods and resources, and have absolutely no need of anything whatsoever….**

Friend, we need to pay attention to this example from Scripture and always keep in mind "Every good gift and every perfect gift is from above, and cometh down from the Father…" (James 1:17). If you are blessed financially, relationally, or spiritually, it is a blessing from God. If you are blessed with material possessions, favorable opportunities, or good health, it is because of Him. You did not arrive where you are or receive what you have on your own. God did it. In fact, He is the One causing your heart to beat and is giving you the very breath you are breathing. Remember, anything good you have — *anything* — is a result of His merciful kindness and grace! Why not take time now to thank Him for His generous provision.

STUDY QUESTIONS

Study to shew thyself approved unto God, a workman that needeth not to be ashamed, rightly dividing the word of truth.
— 2 Timothy 2:15

It is important to note that God is not against anyone being blessed financially or with material possessions. What He is against is the attitude of pride and self-exaltation that can become a snare in our lives when He blesses us. Carefully read Moses' warning to the Israelites in Deuteronomy 8:10-20, just before they crossed into the Promise Land.

According to this passage…

1. What evil tendency must you be mindful of and reject when you experience God's blessings?
2. Who gives you the power to produce wealth? What does God say is its purpose (*see* verse 18)?
3. What does God say will happen if you forget Him?
4. Also consider Proverbs 28:26; Jeremiah 17:5-8; and Philippians 3:3. What is God speaking to you personally through these verses?

PRACTICAL APPLICATION

But be ye doers of the word, and not hearers only, deceiving your own selves.
— James 1:22

1. Think back to a time in your life when you were walking with Jesus and you barely had enough to make ends meet. What was your attitude toward God during those lean days? How did you respond to the blessings of God when they showed up when you needed them most?
2. Have you ever experienced a time of *great success* and *abundant provisions*? Take a moment to briefly describe what it was like. What was your attitude toward God? How did you view His blessings in your

life? Did you see them as a gift from Him or a result of your own ingenuity and ability?

3. What is God revealing to you from the example of the church in Laodicea — who proclaimed to be rich, self-resourced, and in need of nothing? What lesson(s) can you learn and apply in your own life as well as share with family and friends?

TOPIC

Spirituality Poor

SCRIPTURES

1. **Revelation 3:14-17** — And unto the angel of the church of the Laodiceans write; These things saith the Amen, the faithful and true witness, the beginning of the creation of God; I know thy works, that thou art neither cold nor hot: I would thou wert cold or hot. So then because thou art lukewarm, and neither cold nor hot, I will spue thee out of my mouth. Because thou sayest, I am rich, and increased with goods, and have need of nothing; and knowest not that thou art wretched, and miserable, and poor, and blind, and naked.

GREEK WORDS

1. "because" — ὅτι (*hoti*): specifically; in context, points to what Christ has concluded about them
2. "thou sayest" — λέγεις (*legeis*): you allege; you say; not necessarily based on fact, but expresses their flawed opinion of themselves
3. "that" — ὅτι (*hoti*): in context, points to what they are claiming about themselves
4. "I am" — εἰμι (*eimi*): I am; points to self-reliance, self-focus, self-centeredness, even self-absorption; indicates they are the center of their world
5. "rich" — Πλούσιός (*Plousios*): wealth so great it cannot be tabulated; abundant or vast wealth; extreme riches; unlimited wealth; incredible abundance; opulence; extravagant lavishness; someone who possesses

incredible abundance, extreme wealth, and enormous affluence; magnificent wealth; here it is capitalized, possibly meaning "the Richest"

6. "increased with goods" — **πεπλούτηκα** (*peploutika*): from **πλουτέω** (*plouteo*), rich, endowed with resources; in this text, I have made myself rich; I have resourced myself

7. "need of nothing" — **οὐδὲν χρείαν** (*ouden chreian*): the word **οὐδὲν** (*ouden*) means "absolutely nothing"; the word **χρείαν** (*chreian*) depicts a need or deficit; together, absolutely no need of anything whatsoever

8. "have" — **ἔχω** (*echo*): have; hold; possess

9. "knowest not" — **οὐκ οἶδας** (*ouk oidas*): the word **οὐκ** (*ouk*) and **οἶδας** (*oidas*); the word **οὐκ** (*ouk*) is emphatic; emphatically not; the word from **οἶδα** (*oida*) means to see, perceive, understand, or comprehend; together, they denote total lack of comprehension; "you emphatically do not see, perceive, understand, or comprehend"

10. "thou art" — **σὺ εἶ** (*su ei*): the word **σὺ** (*su*) is direct to them; this is a confrontation as Christ directly confronts them with what He sees and knows to be true about them

11. "wretched" — **ὁ ταλαίπωρος** (*ho talaiporos*): definite article **ὁ** (*ho*) with **ταλαίπωρος** (*talaiporos*); the word **ταλαίπωρος** (*talaiporos*) is calloused; negatively affected; in a calloused condition; the definite article means THE most miserable and calloused of everyone

12. "miserable" — **ἐλεεινός** (*eleeinos*): in need of pity; pitiful; to be pitied

13. "poor" — **πτωχὸς** (*ptochos*): not merely poor, but the poorest of all; this was the lowest category of all poor people; destitute and impoverished

14. "blind" — **τυφλὸς** (*tuphlos*): blind; it doesn't just depict a person who is unable to see, but a person who has been intentionally blinded by someone else; one whose eyes have been deliberately removed so that he is blinded; this individual hasn't just lost his sight, but he has no eyes to see

15. "naked" — **γυμνός** (*gumnos*): completely naked

SYNOPSIS

We have seen that Laodicea was once a booming center of commerce and trade that served as the banking center of the Lycus Valley. A series of recent excavations has unearthed the remains of massive buildings, including the ruins of four marketplaces, two theaters, a medical school, and a stadium that seated more than 60,000 people. The remnants of these exquisite carvings, giant columns, and numerous fountains all point to the vastness of Laodicea's former wealth.

The city's First-Century residents were well aware of their great wealth, and it seems that the church in Laodicea was sharing in the great prosperity. Regrettably, they let the glamor of their riches go to their heads. They said, "…I am rich, and increased with goods, and have need of nothing…." Yet, Jesus told them they were "…wretched, and miserable, and poor, and blind, and naked" (Revelation 3:17). Although they were abundantly blessed in the natural, spiritually they were dirt poor.

The emphasis of this lesson:

Although Laodicea was exceedingly rich in material goods and finances, they were exceedingly poor spiritually. Their arrogance and conceit removed their ability to see just how wretched, miserable, and destitute they had become.

Laodicea Had a Water Problem

It is interesting to note that despite their profuse prosperity, Laodicea had a major water problem. Geographically it only had one small brook, which was simply not enough water to meet the needs of the city's residents. To overcome this challenge, the people decided to do something no other city had yet done — they paid for the construction of a system that would transport cold running water and hot running water into their city.

Colossae was a resort town located about nine miles to the southeast of Laodicea, and it was known for its freezing-cold waters. As the snow on the mountains melted, water flowed down filling streams and tributaries. People came from miles around during the hot summer months to be refreshed and revitalized by the ice-cold waters.

Six miles north of Laodicea was the city of Hierapolis, and it was the popular place to be during the cold winter months. Swarms of tourists and Roman soldiers made their way to Hierapolis to bask in the city's renowned hot mineral springs, as they believed the waters had healing properties.

Using their vast resources, the leaders of Laodicea commissioned engineers to build an aqueduct from Colossae and a pipeline from Hierapolis to transport the cold and hot waters into their city. For years the people waited with great anticipation for the work to be completed. Finally, the day came when the systems were done and the people of Laodicea could sample the waters. Unfortunately, by the time the waters arrived from Colossae and Hierapolis, both were lukewarm. Even worse was the taste. After traveling several miles through the clay pipes, the waters had picked up the taste of the minerals and become putrid.

Understanding the 'Neither Cold Nor Hot' Connection

In Revelation 3:15, Jesus told the believers at the church of Laodicea, "I know thy works, that thou art neither cold nor hot: I would thou wert cold or hot." Jesus used the wording "neither cold nor hot" so the people of Laodicea could easily identify with and understand what He was saying. For years they had longed for the ice-cold waters of Colossae and the hot medicinal waters of Hierapolis, but by the time the pipelines were built and they tasted the water for the first time, their expectations were dashed to pieces. The cold water was no longer cold, and the hot water was no longer hot. Both had become lukewarm and made the people want to vomit.

Jesus continued, "So then because thou art lukewarm, and neither cold nor hot, I will spue thee out of my mouth" (Revelation 3:16). In Greek, the phrase "so then because" means *consequently, here is where we're headed*. If they were neither cold nor hot, they could only be "lukewarm," which is the Greek word *chliaros*, describing *something tepid; indifferent; having lost temperature and it has thereby lost value*.

The Laodicean believers had lost their spiritual value. They were no longer refreshing like the freezing-cold waters of Colossae, nor did they have the healing properties of the hot mineral waters of Hierapolis. Jesus hoped and wished that they would return to what they once were. Their lukewarm condition was disgusting to His taste, which is why He was going to "spue" them out of His mouth.

The words "spue thee" in Greek is *se emesai*, which means *to throw up* or *to reject something because its taste is disgusting*. To be clear, Jesus was not rejecting the church of Laodicea, nor was He throwing the believers out of the family of God. He was simply telling them they had lost the revitalizing qualities they once had, and as a result their fellowship was no longer enjoyable to Him.

Laodicea's Exaggerated Opinion of Itself

When we come to Revelation 3:17, Jesus tells us what the believers in Laodicea were saying about themselves. He said, "Because thou sayest, I am rich, and increased with goods, and have need of nothing…." The word "because" is the Greek word *hoti*, which is often translated as the word *that*. Here it points to *something very specific* — something Jesus had observed about them from personally walking in their midst.

He began by saying, "…thou sayest…," which in Greek is the word *legeis*, and it means *you allege* or *you say*. It is *something not necessarily based on fact*, but expresses the Laodicean's flawed opinion of themselves. The truth is, it doesn't really matter what we think or say about ourselves, because apart from God, our hearts are wicked and can deceive us (*see* Jeremiah 17:9). What matters is what Jesus thinks and says about us. He sees everything with pinpoint accuracy and is able to reveal to us what needs to change — and gives us the power to make those changes.

The church of Laodicea was bragging and saying, "…I am rich, and increased with goods, and have need of nothing…." The words "I am" in Greek is a translation of the word *eimi*, which means *I am*. It carries the idea of *self-reliance, self-focus, self-dependence*, and *even self-absorption*. It indicates that the Laodiceans had become *the center of their world*. They were living in a bubble, totally unaware of what was happening to the people around them.

The word "rich" is the Greek word *Plousios*, and it describes *wealth so great it cannot be tabulated; extreme riches; incredible abundance; opulence; extravagant lavishness*. This word denotes *someone who possesses extreme wealth and enormous affluence*. What is interesting is that in this verse, the word *Plousios* is capitalized, which likely indicates that the Laodiceans believed they were *the Richest* church of all.

At that time, Laodicea may have been the richest of all the cities in the Roman Empire. It certainly was the richest city in the Lycus Valley. They said they were "increased with goods," which is the Greek word *peploutika*, from the word *plouteo*, meaning *rich, endowed with resources*. In context here, it is the equivalent of saying, "I have made myself rich; I have resourced myself." It was this arrogant attitude of pride and self-reliance that Jesus was against. It's true that Laodicea had been abundantly blessed, but the blessings came from God — not from the people themselves.

Furthermore, the Laodicean believers said, "…[we] have need of nothing." The word "have" is the Greek word *echo*, which means *to have, hold, or possess*. And the phrase "need of nothing" is a translation of the Greek words *ouden cheiran*. The word *ouden* means *absolutely nothing*, and the word *cheiran* depicts *a need or deficit*. When these words are joined, it means *absolutely no need of anything whatsoever*.

Putting the meanings of all these words together, here is the *Renner Interpretive Version (RIV)* of the first part of Revelation 3:17:

Because you keep on bragging, I am rich, wealthy, influential, the Richest of all, and I have endowed myself with vast goods and resources, and have absolutely no need of anything whatsoever….

The Real Condition of the Church of Laodicea

In the second half of Revelation 3:17, Jesus went on to say, "…and knowest not that thou art wretched, and miserable, and poor, and blind, and naked." This portion of Scripture is simply packed with meaning.

For instance notice the words "knowest not." In Greek it is *ouk oidas*. The word *ouk* is emphatic, meaning *emphatically not*. The word *oidas* is from *oida*, which means *to see, perceive, understand, or comprehend*. Taken together, *ouk oidas* denotes *total lack of comprehension*. It is the equivalent of saying, "You emphatically do not see, perceive, understand, or comprehend."

'Wretched'

What did the Laodicean church emphatically not know? They did not know they were "…wretched, and miserable, and poor, and blind, and naked." The word "wretched" in Greek is *ho talaiporos*. *Ho* is a definite article, and the word *talaiporos* means *calloused; negatively affected;* or *in a calloused condition*. The fact that there is a definite article attached here indicates that the Laodicean church was *THE most miserable and calloused of everyone*.

'Miserable, Poor, Blind, and Naked'

The word "miserable" is the Greek word *eleeinos*, which means *in need of pity; pitiful; to be pitied*. The word "poor" in Greek is *ptochos*, which describes *not merely poor*, but *the poorest of all*. This was *the lowest category of all poor people*. "Blind" is a translation of the word *tuphlos*, and it doesn't just depict a person who is unable to see, but *a person who has been intentionally blinded by someone else*. It is *one whose eyes have been deliberately removed or gouged out so that he is blinded*. This individual hasn't just lost his sight, but he has no eyes to see. Lastly is the word "naked," which in Greek is the word *gumnos*, and it means *completely naked*.

Jesus used all these words to describe the true condition of the church of Laodicea. Although they saw themselves as abundantly rich, increased with goods, and in need of nothing, Jesus saw them as they really were — extremely calloused, extremely poor, completely naked, and totally blind to their true spiritual condition. And because of all this, they were to be pitied. He told them these things not to hurt them or condemn them but to awaken them to the truth in order that they might repent and turn back to Him. In our next lesson, we will focus on the solution Jesus gave to the church in Laodicea as to how to get back on track.

STUDY QUESTIONS

> **Study to shew thyself approved unto God, a workman that needeth not to be ashamed, rightly dividing the word of truth.**
> **— 2 Timothy 2:15**

1. Jesus told the church of Laodicea that they were "wretched," which means *extremely calloused*. Have you ever had a callus? If so, how did it feel compared to where there were no calluses? Knowing that, what do you think happens when you have a spiritual callus?

2. The Bible says, "The heart is hopelessly dark and deceitful, a puzzle that no one can figure out" (Jeremiah 17:9 *MSG*). How can we know the true condition of our hearts? Read Jeremiah 17:10; Proverbs 21:2; and Psalm 139:23,24.

3. Clearly, the heart condition of the church of Laodicea had become hardened and insensitive to the Holy Spirit. If your heart is not as it should be, take time to meditate on God's repeated promise to you in Ezekiel 11:19,20 and 36:26,27. How would you turn these verses into a prayer?

PRACTICAL APPLICATION

But be ye doers of the word, and not hearers only,
deceiving your own selves.
—James 1:22

1. If Jesus were to show up at *your* church and take an inventory of its
    condition, what would He find?

    • In His overall assessment, would He say your church is *hot*? *Cold*?
      Or *lukewarm*?

    • What would He say about your church's *teaching of the Bible*? Is it
      refreshing and *revitalizing*?

    • Would He see the *gifts of the Holy Spirit* in operation and bringing
      healing to people?

    • Consider your church's *hospitality* and *ministry to others*. How do
      they treat orphans, widows, and those sick or in prison?

2. The people in the church of Laodicea saw themselves as *rich, increased
    with goods*, and *in need of nothing*. How do you see yourself? Specifi-
    cally, how would you describe your spiritual condition? Have you ever
    stopped to ask God how He sees you? Take a moment to do that right
    now.

LESSON 5

TOPIC

Christ's Counsel to the Calloused

SCRIPTURES

1. **Revelation 3:14-18** — And unto the angel of the church of the
    Laodiceans write; These things saith the Amen, the faithful and true
    witness, the beginning of the creation of God; I know thy works,
    that thou art neither cold nor hot: I would thou wert cold or hot. So
    then because thou art lukewarm, and neither cold nor hot, I will spue
    thee out of my mouth. Because thou sayest, I am rich, and increased
    with goods, and have need of nothing; and knowest not that thou art
    wretched, and miserable, and poor, and blind, and naked: I counsel

thee to buy of me gold tried in the fire, that thou mayest be rich; and white raiment, that thou mayest be clothed, and that the shame of thy nakedness do not appear; and anoint thine eyes with eyesalve, that thou mayest see.

GREEK WORDS

1. "because" — ὅτι (*hoti*): specifically; in context, points to what Christ has concluded about them

2. "thou sayest" — λέγεις (*legeis*): you allege; you say; not necessarily based on fact, but expresses their flawed opinion of themselves

3. "I am" — εἰμι (*eimi*): I am; points to self-reliance, self-focus, self-centeredness, even self-absorption; indicates they are the center of their world

4. "rich" — Πλούσιός (*Plousios*): wealth so great it cannot be tabulated; abundant or vast wealth; extreme riches; unlimited wealth; incredible abundance; opulence; extravagant lavishness; someone who possesses incredible abundance, extreme wealth, and enormous affluence; magnificent wealth; here it is capitalized, possibly meaning "the Richest"

5. "increased with goods" — πεπλούτηκα (*peploutika*): from πλουτέω (*plouteo*), rich, endowed with resources; in this text, I have made myself rich; I have resourced myself

6. "need of nothing" — οὐδὲν χρείαν (*ouden chreian*): the word οὐδὲν (*ouden*) means "absolutely nothing"; the word χρείαν (*chreian*) depicts a need or deficit; absolutely no need of anything whatsoever

7. "knowest not" — οὐκ οἶδας (*ouk oidas*): the word οὐκ (*ouk*) and οἶδας (*oidas*); the word οὐκ (*ouk*) is emphatic; emphatically not; the word from οἶδα (*oida*) means to see, perceive, understand, or comprehend; together, they denote total lack of comprehension; "you emphatically do not see, perceive, understand, or comprehend"

8. "wretched" — ὁ ταλαίπωρος (*ho talaiporos*): definite article ὁ (*ho*) with ταλαίπωρος (*talaiporos*); the word ταλαίπωρος (*talaiporos*) is calloused, negatively affected; in a calloused condition; the definite article means THE most miserable and calloused of everyone

9. "miserable" — ἐλεεινός (*eleeinos*): in need of pity; pitiful; to be pitied

10. "poor" — πτωχὸς (*ptochos*): not merely poor, but the poorest of all; this was the lowest category of all poor people; destitute and impoverished

11. "blind" — **τυφλὸς** (*tuphlos*): blind; it doesn't just depict a person who is unable to see, but a person who has been intentionally blinded by someone else; one whose eyes have been deliberately removed so that he is blinded; this individual hasn't just lost his sight, but he has no eyes to see

12. "naked" — **γυμνός** (*gumnos*): completely naked

13. "I counsel" — **συμβουλεύω** (*sumbouleuo*): from **σύν** (*sun*) and **βουλεύω** (*bouleuo*); the word **σύν** (*sun*) means "together"; carries the idea of association; to do something jointly with someone else; the word **βουλεύω** (*bouleuo*) means to advise, counsel, or determine; together, it pictures a joint counseling or a joint determination

14. "thee" — **σοι** (*soi*): directly to you; mincing no words; straight to the point

15. "buy" — **ἀγοράζω** (*agoradzo*): to buy; depicts a purchase in the marketplace; to redeem

16. "of me" — **παρ' ἐμοῦ** (*par' emou*): from **παρά** (*para*) meaning alongside; right alongside me; from my side; available only at my side

17. "gold" — **χρυσός** (*chrusos*): pictures gold, the most valuable material that existed in the ancient world; denotes that which is rare and highly prized; used figuratively to denote something precious or of great significance

18. "tried" — **πεπυρωμένον** (*pepuromenon*): from **πυρόω** (*puroo*), to burn; here it means having been fired; having been purified; having been refined; depicts a purification process; to be inflamed

19. "in the fire" — **ἐκ πυρὸς** (*ek puros*) out of fire; a purification that proceeds from fire

20. "rich" — **πλούσιος** (*plousios*): wealth so great it cannot be tabulated; abundant wealth; vast wealth; extreme riches; incredible abundance; used by Plato to say no one was richer than legendary King Midas

21. "white raiment" — **ἱμάτια λευκὰ** (*himatia leuka*): dazzling and resplendent garments; specially important to Laodicea

22. "that" — **ἵνα** (*hina:*) points to purpose; in order that

23. "not appear" — **μὴ φανερωθῇ** (*me phanerothe*): will not become visibly evident

24. "shame" — **αἰσχύνη** (*aischune*): disgrace, embarrassment, or humiliation; degraded, debased, or dishonored

25. "eyesalve" — **κολλούριον** (*kollourion*): ointment to heal the eyes; Laodicea was famous for a healing eye ointment that was renowned all over the ancient world

26. "anoint" — **ἐγχρίω** (*egchrio*): to anoint; here, a command to take action to bring correction to their sight problem

27. "see" — **βλέπω** (*blepo*): to see, behold, or to be aware; often intended to jolt and jar a listener or viewer to perk up and really listen to what is being said or to what is being seen

SYNOPSIS

Located in the city of Laodicea are the remains of a very unique structure that dates back to the year 313 AD. It was one of the first official church buildings erected after the Edict of Toleration was issued by Rome that officially ended the persecution of Christians. In its original state, the facility was about 20,000 square feet, and its architecture — including the beautiful mosaics and detailed reliefs — was magnificent. This building and its décor were yet another confirmation of Laodicea's vast wealth.

Indeed, the church of Laodicea was apparently just as financially blessed as the residents of the city. Their prosperity, however, led to pride and caused them to become blind and calloused to their true spiritual condition. In the natural they were rich, but spiritually they were wretched, miserable, poor, and naked. In His mercy, Jesus not only corrected them but also directed them on what they needed to do to self-correct and make things right.

The emphasis of this lesson:

After Jesus pointed out Laodicea's deplorable spiritual condition, He counseled them on what they needed to do to reestablish a right relationship with Him. He urged them to come to Him and receive all that they needed to be spiritually clothed and truly rich.

Jesus began His message to the church of Laodicea saying, "And unto the angel of the church of the Laodiceans write; These things saith the Amen, the faithful and true witness, the beginning of the creation of God" (Revelation 3:14). Here, Christ identified Himself as *the Amen*, meaning He is the final word on every subject, including your health, your finances, your family, and your future.

He then said, "I know thy works, that thou art neither cold nor hot: I would thou wert cold or hot. So then because thou art lukewarm, and neither cold nor hot, I will spue thee out of my mouth" (Revelation 3:15, 16). We have seen that the word "lukewarm" in Greek is the word *chliaros*, which means *tepid* or *indifferent*. It speaks of *a loss of temperature*, and therefore it indicates *a loss of value*. And the word "spue" is the Greek word *emesai*, from the word *emeo*, which means *to vomit; to throw up; or to reject something because its taste is disgusting.*

In these verses, Jesus basically tells the Laodicean believers, "You are no longer hot with medicinal value, neither are you cold and refreshing as you once were. When I taste of your fellowship, it is blasé — empty of passion, and putrid. And because you're lukewarm, I'm going to spue you out of My mouth."

Laodicea Had a Skewed View of Themselves

In Revelation 3:17, Jesus quoted back to the church of Laodicea what they had been saying about themselves. He said, "Because thou sayest, I am rich, and increased with goods, and have need of nothing; and knowest not that thou art wretched, and miserable, and poor, and blind, and naked...." Let's review the key words in this verse to solidify in our hearts what Jesus was actually communicating.

First, Jesus used the word "because," which in Greek is the word *hoti*, and points to *a very specific conclusion* Jesus came to about them. Remember, He had been walking up and down in the midst of all the churches (*see* Revelation 2:1), and He "knew" (*oida*) from personal observation, all their *deeds*, *actions*, and *activities* (*erga*). Now He was going to give them an accurate analysis of their true condition.

He said, "thou sayest," which in Greek is the word *legeis*. The phrase "Because thou sayest" could be translated "Because you are *asserting*," "Because you're *alleging*," or "Because you are *bragging*...." Like the Laodicean church, the things that we assert or allege about ourselves are often not factual and can even be delusional. The only thing that matters is what Jesus sees and says about us.

The believers in Laodicea were saying, "...I am rich, and increased with goods, and have need of nothing...." We've seen that the words "I am" are a translation of the Greek word *eimi*, which signifies *self-reliance, self-focus*, and *self-centeredness*. This means they really weren't looking to and relying on the Lord, nor were they considering the people around them. They had become the center of their world.

From all indications, it seems that the Laodicean believers lived in a bubble. They were unaware that the church in Colossae and the church in Hierapolis were experiencing persecution. Fully engrossed in themselves, they said, "…I am rich, and increased with goods, and have need of nothing…." The word "rich" is the Greek word *Plousios*, which describes *extreme riches, incredible abundance, and wealth so great it cannot be tabulated.* In this verse, *Plousios* is capitalized, which possibly means they saw themselves as "the Richest" of all the churches.

The church of Laodicea also said they were "increased with goods," which in the Greek text here means *I have made myself rich; I have resourced myself.* Moreover, they declared they had "need of nothing," which means they believed they had *absolutely no need of anything whatsoever.*

Jesus Revealed Laodicea's Wretched Spiritual Condition

Not wanting to leave the Laodicean believers in the darkness of self-deception, Jesus pulled back the curtains and revealed to them their true spiritual condition. He said, "…and knowest not that thou art wretched, and miserable, and poor, and blind, and naked" (Revelation 3:17).

"Knowest not" in Greek is *ouk oidas.* The word *ouk* means *emphatically not*, and the word *oidas* is from *oida*, which means *to see, perceive, understand,* or *comprehend.* Together, *ouk oidas* indicates *a total lack of comprehension.* It is the same as Jesus saying, "You emphatically do not see, perceive, understand, or comprehend."

Blinded by pride, the Laodicean church emphatically did not know that they were "wretched, and poor, and blind, and naked." The word "wretched" in Greek is *ho talaiporos.* The word *talaiporos* means *calloused; negatively affected;* or *in a calloused condition,* and *ho* is a definite article signifying that the Laodicean church was *THE most miserable and calloused of everyone.*

The word "miserable" is the Greek word *eleeinos*, which means they were *to be pitied* because their condition was so dreadful. The word "poor" in Greek is *ptochos*, which describes *abject poverty — the lowest category of all poor people.* "Blind" is a translation of the word *tuphlos*, and it depicts *a person* who has been intentionally blinded by someone else; one whose eyes have been deliberately removed or gouged out so that he is blinded. This individual hasn't just lost his sight — he has no eyes to see.

Lastly, Jesus said the Laodicean church was "naked," which in Greek is the word *gumnos*, and it means *completely naked*. This was a very strange statement to tell people who were rich in material possessions and lived sumptuous lifestyles. Yet it was the truth. Although they were adorned in lavish clothes, spiritually they were completely naked.

Jesus' Counsel: 'Buy from Me What You Can't Buy Anywhere Else'

In Revelation 3:18, Jesus — the Great Physician — gave the church in Laodicea a cure for their calloused heart. He said, "I counsel thee to buy of me gold tried in the fire, that thou mayest be rich…." The words "I counsel" in Greek is *sumbouleuo*, which is from the words *sun* and *bouleuo*. The word *sun* means "together" and carries the idea of *association; to do something jointly with someone else*. The word *bouleuo* means *to advise, counsel, or determine*. When compounded, the word *sumbouleuo* — translated here as "I counsel" — pictures *a joint counseling or a joint determination*.

When Jesus said "I counsel thee," it was the equivalent of Him saying, "Hey, let's you and Me come together and make a decision on how to fix things." The word "thee" in Greek is *soi*, which indicates He was *coming directly to them*, *mincing no words*, and *getting straight to the point*. To be clear, Jesus did not condemn them. He confronted them in love — and offered them counsel and a willingness to work with them to get them back into a healthy spiritual state.

What was Jesus' counsel? He said, "…buy of me gold tried in the fire, that thou mayest be rich…." The word "buy" is the Greek word *agoradzo*, which means *to buy* and depicts *a purchase in the marketplace*. It is also the word for *redemption*. Keep in mind the Laodiceans had four large marketplaces and about 4,500 small shops — all of them teeming with products. Indeed, there was a lot of shopping going on, but not one of those shops had what the church needed. Basically Jesus told believers, "You need something that can't be bought in any marketplace or shop; it is gold that only comes from Me."

"Gold" is the Greek word *chrusos*, and it pictures *gold, the most valuable material that existed in the ancient world.* It also denotes *that which is rare and highly prized.* The word *chrusos* can also be used figuratively to indicate *something precious* or *of great significance.* The gold Jesus offers has been "tried by fire." The word "tried" here is the Greek word *pepuromenon*, which is from *puroo*, meaning *to burn.* In context, it means *having been fired; having been purified; having been refined.* It depicts *a purification process.*

This brings us to the phrase "in the fire," which is *ek puros* in Greek, meaning *out of fire.* It describes *a purification that proceeds from fire.* Some people who have read this believe it means they must go through extreme difficulties in order to be purified, but that is not what Jesus was saying. Yes, fire was used for purification purposes. But it was also used to *burn rubbish* and *empower engines,* making it a source of energy. With this in mind, let's look again at Jesus' interaction with the church of Laodicea and get the "big picture" of what He was saying.

In essence, Jesus told His Church:

> "You have an issue of pride. You arrogantly think your abundance of goods and level of success is the result of your own hands — that you've resourced yourself and made yourself great. The truth is, you are spiritually wretched, miserable, poor, and naked. Your conceit has blinded you and made you calloused to your true condition. Regardless of how much money you have or the number of material possessions you own, you are spiritually bankrupt.

> Therefore, come to Me! I'm the marketplace of true riches. I'm loaded with everything you need — including the finest, most expensive gold. What I give to you is like divine fire. It will burn the garbage and nonsense of this world out of you, purifying and empowering you like fire always does. My desire is that you not just be rich in the natural, but also be rich spiritually."

Jesus' Purpose: 'That You May Be Spiritually Rich and Clothed'

Why did Jesus want the church in Laodicea — *and us* — to buy from Him gold that is tried by fire? The Bible says, "…that thou mayest be rich…" (Revelation 3:18). The word "rich" here is again the Greek word *plousios,* which describes *wealth so great it cannot be tabulated.* This was the same word used for a *plutocrat* or *one who was filthy, stinking rich.* The use of this word lets us know that Jesus is not against a person being abundantly blessed. Having material blessings is a part of redemption. What He is against is a person who is richly blessed and arrogantly thinking he has achieved it on his own. "Always remember that it is the Lord your God who gives you power to become rich…" (Deuteronomy 8:18 *TLB*).

In addition to gold tried in the fire, Jesus told the Laodicean church to buy "white raiment." This is the phrase *himatia leuka* in Greek, and it describes *dazzling and resplendent garments.* Jesus doesn't just want His Church to be decked out in the natural. He wants us to be clothed in regal attire spiritually. And by doing so, the shame of our nakedness will "not appear" (*see* Revelation 3:18).

In Greek, the words "not appear" is a translation of the phrase *me phanerothe*, and it means shame *will not become visibly evident.* "Shame" is the Greek word *aischune*, and it describes *disgrace, embarrassment, or humiliation.* It carries the idea of being *degraded, debased, or dishonored.* Essentially, Jesus is saying, "I don't want anyone to see your debased and degraded condition. I want it to be covered in the dazzling robe of righteousness I have made available to you." Make no mistake: Jesus is never in a rush to publicly expose a person's sins.

Jesus Has the Anointed Ointment To Open Our Spiritual Eyes

The last instruction He gave the Laodicean believers in verse 18 was "… anoint thine eyes with eyesalve, that thou mayest see." The word "anoint" in Greek is *egchrio*, and it means *to anoint.* In this case, it is *a command to take action and bring correction to their sight problem.* The word "eyesalve" is the Greek word *kollourion*, and it describes *ointment to heal the eyes.* It is actually the same word used for the Phrygian eye salve produced in Laodicea that was famous all over the ancient world for its healing properties. Here again, Jesus used an illustration from the local culture to enable His people to grab hold of what He was saying. Basically He said, "Just as you have a medical school that produces medicine to heal sick eyes, I have a special medicine that will open and heal your spiritual eyes."

Jesus said the spiritual eye salve He offered would help them "see" again. In Greek, the word "see" is *blepo*, which means *to see, behold, or to be aware.* This word is often intended to jolt and jar a listener or viewer to perk up and really listen to what is being said or to what is being seen. Hence for the eyes of the Laodicean believers to be opened and their sight restored, they needed to come to Jesus — the Source of the anointing. He had everything they needed.

STUDY QUESTIONS

Study to shew thyself approved unto God, a workman that needeth
not to be ashamed, rightly dividing the word of truth.
— 2 Timothy 2:15

1. When Jesus revealed the true spiritual condition of the church in Laodicea, it was not to condemn them. The same is true for you. Whenever He shows you something in your life that is not in line with His Word, it is always for the purpose of working with you to change it. What message of encouragement is God communicating to you in these passages?
    *   **Romans 8:1,2 and 8:31-39**
    *   **John 3:17,18**
    *   **1 John 3:19-22**

2. The Bible says, "For whom he did foreknow, he also did predestinate to be conformed to the image of his Son…" (Romans 8:29). This conforming is the *process of purification* that all believers take part in. God, through the indwelling Person of the Holy Spirit, plays a major part in your purification. Carefully read these verses and identify *His* part and *your* part.
    *   **Philippians 1:6 and 2:12,13**
    *   **1 Thessalonians 5:23,24**
    *   **2 Corinthians 3:16-18**
    *   **Hebrews 13:20,21**

PRACTICAL APPLICATION

But be ye doers of the word, and not hearers only,
deceiving your own selves.
— James 1:22

Jesus told the believers in Laodicea, "You need something that can't be bought in any marketplace or shop; it is 'gold' — something exceedingly precious and rare — that only comes from Me."

1. Are you experiencing a sense of emptiness in your life — does something seem to be missing, but you don't know what it is? What steps have you taken to fill the void?

2. Take time right now to sit in God's presence and pour your heart out to Him (*see* Psalm 62:8). Ask Him to show you the precious and rare "gold" that is missing from your life. Then ask Him to provide it.

3. Jesus also wants to restore your spiritual vision so you can see things the way He sees them. Take time and pray: *"Lord, please forgive me for being proud in any way or thinking that the blessings in my life came to me because of something I did. Give me spiritual eyes that see, spiritual ears that hear, and a tender heart that responds in obedience to You."*

LESSON 6

TOPIC

Christ's Rebuke and Chastening of His Church

SCRIPTURES

1. **Revelation 3:14-19** — And unto the angel of the church of the Laodiceans write; These things saith the Amen, the faithful and true witness, the beginning of the creation of God; I know thy works, that thou art neither cold nor hot: I would thou wert cold or hot. So then because thou art lukewarm, and neither cold nor hot, I will spue thee out of my mouth. Because thou sayest, I am rich, and increased with goods, and have need of nothing; and knowest not that thou art wretched, and miserable, and poor, and blind, and naked: I counsel thee to buy of me gold tried in the fire, that thou mayest be rich; and white raiment, that thou mayest be clothed, and that the shame of thy nakedness do not appear; and anoint thine eyes with eyesalve, that thou mayest see. As many as I love, I rebuke and chasten: be zealous therefore, and repent.

GREEK WORDS

1. "I counsel" — **συμβουλεύω** (*sumbouleuo*): from **σύν** (*sun*) and **βουλεύω** (*bouleuo*); the word **σύν** (*sun*) means "together"; carries the idea of association; to do something jointly with someone else; the word **βουλεύω** (*bouleuo*) means to advise, counsel, or determine; together, it pictures a joint counseling or a joint determination

2. "thee" — **σοι** (*soi*): directly to you; mincing no words; straight to the point

3. "buy" — **ἀγοράζω** (*agoradzo*): to buy; depicts a purchase in the marketplace; to redeem

4. "of me" — **παρ' ἐμοῦ** (*par' emou*): from **παρά** (*para*) meaning alongside; right alongside me; from my side; available only at my side

5. "gold" — **χρυσός** (*chrusos*): pictures gold, the most valuable material that existed in the ancient world; denotes that which is rare and highly prized; used figuratively to denote something precious or of great significance

6. "tried" — **πεπυρωμένον** (*pepuromenon*): from **πυρόω** (*puroo*), to burn; here it means having been fired; having been purified; having been refined; depicts a purification process; to be inflamed

7. "in the fire" — **ἐκ πυρὸς** (*ek puros*): out of fire; a purification that proceeds from fire

8. "rich" — **πλούσιος** (*plousios*): wealth so great it cannot be tabulated; abundant wealth; vast wealth; extreme riches; incredible abundance; used by Plato to say no one was richer than legendary King Midas

9. "white raiment" — **ἱμάτια λευκὰ** (*himatia leuka*): dazzling and resplendent garments; specially important to Laodicea

10. "clothed" — **περιβάλλω** (*periballo*): enrobed; wrapped around

11. "not appear" — **μὴ φανερωθῇ** (*me phanerothe*): will not become visibly evident

12. "shame" — **αἰσχύνη** (*aischune*): disgrace, embarrassment, or humiliation; degraded, debased, or dishonored

13. "anoint" — **ἐγχρίω** (*egchrio*): to anoint; here, a command to take action to bring correction to their sight problem

14. "eyesalve" — **κολλούριον** (*kollourion*): ointment to heal the eyes

15. "see" — βλέπω (*blepo*): to see, behold, or to be aware; often intended to jolt and jar a listener or viewer to perk up and really listen to what is being said or to what is being seen

16. "I" — ἐγὼ (*ego*): He used this word repeatedly to draw attention to Himself

17. "if" — εάν (*ean*): if; should

18. "if I love" — ἐὰν ἐγὼ φιλῶ (*ean ego philo*): the word ἐὰν (*ean*) means "if" and states this is how Christ deals with those He loves; the word φιλῶ (*philo*) is from φιλέω (*phileo*) and depicts affection, fondness, or real love; together, "if I love with a genuine love"

19. "I rebuke" — ἐλέγχω (*elegcho*): to expose, convict, or cross-examine for the purpose of conviction, as when convicting a lawbreaker in a court of law; pictures a lawyer who brings evidence that is indisputable and undeniable, so the accused person's actions are irrefutably brought to light and the offender is exposed and convicted; used in a positive sense to convince someone of something; denotes a lawyer who worked diligently to convince people of a new way of thinking or a new way of seeing things

20. "I chasten" — παιδεύω (*paideuo*): I teach and train; to train children, or anyone, with strict discipline to help them mature and become responsible adults; to assist one in reaching full potential

21. "be zealous" — ζηλόω (*zeloo*): to be heated or to boil; enthusiasm, fervor, passion, devotion, or an eagerness to achieve something; to be deeply committed to something; even to be moved with envy, hatred, anger

22. "therefore" — οὖν (*oun*): consequently

23. "repent" — μετανοέω (*metanoeo*): a change of mind that results in a complete, radical, total change of behavior; a decision to completely change or to entirely turn around in the way that one is thinking, believing, or living; to entirely turn around; a total transformation affecting every part of a person's life, both inside and outside, resulting in a behavioral change

SYNOPSIS

As we have seen, the city of Laodicea was fabulously rich. In fact, it was the richest city in the entire Lycus Valley and possibly the richest in the entire Roman Empire. History reveals that Laodicea suffered a catastrophic earthquake during the First Century that decimated the city. When Rome offered to help finance its rebuilding, the people of Laodicea rejected it. Essentially, the Laodiceans proclaimed, "We are Laodicea. We are exceedingly rich and don't need anyone's help."

What's interesting is that this ardent self-reliance was also prevalent in the church of Laodicea. According to Revelation 3:17, the believers saw themselves as *rich, increased with goods*, and *in need of nothing*. But Jesus saw their true condition, and because He loved them so much, He chose to "rebuke and chasten" them (*see* Revelation 3:19). Along with giving them some specific action steps to self-correct, He called them to "be zealous, therefore, and repent" (Revelation 3:19).

The emphasis of this lesson:

The reason Jesus rebuked and chastened the church of Laodicea was to lead them to repentance and get them back on track. It's the same reason He reprimands and corrects us. His motivation is always love with the hope of reestablishing us in right relationship with Him.

A Review of What We've Learned
Revelation 3:14-17

It was to the apostle John, who had been imprisoned on the Isle of Patmos, that Jesus gave a vivid revelation of Himself and revealed future events that were yet to take place. As the Lord made known His revelation to John, He included a message to each of the seven major churches on the continent of Asia. The church in Laodicea was one of them.

He said, "And unto the angel of the church of the Laodiceans write; These things saith the Amen, the faithful and true witness, the beginning of the creation of God; I know thy works, that thou art neither cold nor hot: I would thou wert cold or hot. So then because thou art lukewarm, and neither cold nor hot, I will spue thee out of my mouth" (Revelation 3:14-16).

We have noted in previous lessons that Jesus was fully aware of everything going on in the church of Laodicea. He had been walking in the very midst of each of the seven churches and had personally observed all their activities, actions, and deeds. The believers in Laodicea were no longer refreshing, neither were they providing the revitalizing healing they once did when the church was first birthed. They had become *indifferent* in their devotion to Jesus, and their fellowship was now nauseating to Him. Hence, he told them He was going to vomit them out of His mouth.

The Laodiceans were very wealthy, and as a result, they developed an attitude of pride and self-reliance. Jesus clearly exposed this to them in Revelation 3:17, saying, "Because thou sayest, I am rich, and increased with goods, and have need of nothing; and knowest not that thou art wretched, and miserable, and poor, and blind, and naked" (Revelation 3:17).

We have seen that the phrase "because thou sayest" in Greek specifically points to something the Laodicean believers were *alleging* about themselves. They had become *self-centered* and *self-focused* — bragging about how rich they were. But their view was incorrect and not based on fact.

Blinded by pride, the church of Laodicea said they were...

"Rich" — the Greek word *Plousios* describes *wealth so great it cannot be tabulated; abundant or vast wealth; extreme riches.* Here the word *Plousios* is capitalized, possibly indicating that the Laodicean church believed it was *The Richest* of all the churches, which may very well have been true.

"Increased with Goods" — the Greek word *peploutika*, which is from the word *plouteo*, meaning *rich, endowed with resources.* In this verse, it specifically means *I have made myself rich; I have resourced myself.*

"[In] Need of Nothing" — the Greek words *ouden cheiran.* The word *ouden* means *absolutely nothing*; the word *cheiran* depicts *a need or deficit.* When the two words are joined together, it means *absolutely no need of anything whatsoever.*

Jesus — the Truth-Detector — told the Laodiceans they were...

"Wretched" — a translation of the Greek words *ho talaiporos.* The word *talaiporos* means *calloused, negatively affected; in a calloused condition.* Because the definite article *ho* is included, it is the equivalent of Jesus saying the Laodicean believers were *THE most miserable and calloused of everyone.*

"Miserable" — the Greek word *eleeinos*, which means *in need of pity*. By using this word, Jesus was saying, "You are *to be pitied* for how deplorable your condition is."

"Poor" — the Greek word *ptochos*, which means *not merely poor*, but *the poorest of all*. Although the church in Laodicea was abundantly rich in the natural, spiritually they were living in *abject poverty — destitute and impoverished*.

"Blind" — a translation of the Greek word *tuphlos*. This doesn't just depict a person who is blind and unable to see, but *a person who has been intentionally blinded by someone else*. It is *one whose eyes have been deliberately gouged out or removed so that he is blinded; he has no eyes to see*.

"Naked" — from the Greek word *gumnos*, meaning *completely naked*. Physically, the Laodicean believers were lavishly dressed, but in the spirit they were *totally uncovered* and *vulnerable*.

Jesus Offers the Remedy for His Sick Church

In Revelation 3:18, Jesus said, "I counsel thee to buy of me gold tried in the fire, that thou mayest be rich; and white raiment, that thou mayest be clothed, and that the shame of thy nakedness do not appear; and anoint thine eyes with eyesalve, that thou mayest see."

In our last lesson, we saw that the phrase "I counsel" in Greek is *sumbouleuo*, which is from the words *sun* and *bouleuo*. The word *sun* carries the idea of *association; to do something jointly with someone else*. The word *bouleuo* means *to advise, to counsel, or to determine*. When compounded, the word *sumbouleuo* describes *a joint decision to take action*. Thus, when Jesus said "I counsel thee," it was the same as Him saying, "Hey, let's you and Me get together and make a decision on how to fix this situation." The word "thee" in Greek is *soi*, which indicates that Jesus is *speaking candidly to the church, not mincing words*.

"Buy of me gold tried in the fire." Jesus got straight to the point. When He said "buy," He used the word *agoradzo* in Greek, which means *to buy* and depicts *a purchase in the marketplace*. It is also the word for *redemption*. Remember, Laodicea had four large marketplaces and about 4,500 small shops packed with products from all over the world. By using this word, Jesus was indirectly saying, "Forget about all the marketplaces and shops around you. I am the marketplace you need — I offer the resources no one else is selling."

"Gold" was *the most expensive commodity in the ancient world.* The word "gold" here is the Greek word *chrusos*, which was *the rarest, purest gold available.* This word is used to denote *that which is rare and highly prized.* Figuratively, it indicates *something precious* or *of great significance.* The gold Jesus offers has been "tried in the fire." The word "tried" is the Greek word *pepuromenon*, which is from *puroo*, meaning *to burn.* In context, it means *having been fired; having been purified; having been refined.* It depicts *a purification process.*

"In the fire." In Greek, this phrase is *ek puros*, which means *straight out of the fire.* Now some who have read this passage have misinterpreted Jesus' words to mean they have to go through extreme trials in order to be purified, but that is not what He was saying. We must understand that fire was used for several reasons. First, it was used to *burn rubbish.* Second, it was used *to purify.* Third, fire was used to *empower engines and machinery.* These uses for fire help us see more accurately what Jesus said to the church in Laodicea and to us. Essentially, He said, "Come to Me and receive the fire you need to *incinerate* the worthless chaff out of your life. The fire I provide will get rid of your pride and calloused condition. It will *purify* you and *empower* you to get back on track with Me."

The Reward for Our Obedience: We Will Be Spiritually 'Rich' and 'Clothed'

After Jesus said to buy from Him *gold tried in the fire*, He announced the rewards for obeying His instructions. He said, "…that thou mayest be rich; and [buy] white raiment, that thou mayest be clothed, and that the shame of thy nakedness do not appear…" (Revelation 3:18). The word "rich" here is again the Greek word *plousios*, which is *wealth so great it cannot be tabulated.* Clearly, Jesus wants us to be rich — but not just rich in the natural. He desires us to be rich *spiritually.*

Being clothed in "white raiment" is a rich spiritual blessing. In Greek, the words "white raiment" is *himatia leuka*, which depicts *dazzling and resplendent garments.* The Bible says when we are spiritually clothed in white raiment, the "shame" of our nakedness does "not appear." "Shame" in Greek is the word *aischune*, and it describes *disgrace, embarrassment, or humiliation.* And the phrase "not appear" is *me phanerothe*, which means *will not become visibly evident.*

Essentially, in this part of verse 18, Jesus said, "I don't want anyone else to see the areas of your life that are *embarrassing, degrading, and humiliating.* That's why I'm counseling you to buy white raiment from Me. These dazzling spiritual garments will cover your shame. When you come to Me, I will get involved, and we will work together to resolve this situation."

Love Is Always the Motivating Factor in Christ's Correction

Revelation 3:19 says, "As many as I love, I rebuke and chasten: be zealous therefore, and repent." What is very interesting and important to note is that in the original Greek, this verse appears quite differently. It begins, "[I] as many as [if] I love, I rebuke and [I] chasten...." Let's unpack the meaning of this passage by observing some key words.

First, notice the word "I." It is the Greek word *ego*, and while it means *I*, it *emphatically draws attention to Jesus Himself.* It is the equivalent of Jesus saying, "*I* am now going to tell you how *I* deal with people who need correction."

Next is the word "if," which is the Greek word *ean*, and it means *if* or *should.* Thus, Jesus said, "*If* I love..." The phrase "I love" in Greek is *ean philo.* Again, the word *ean* means *if*, and states *this is how Christ deals with those whom He loves.* The word *philo* is from *phileo* and depicts *affection, fondness*, or *real love.* When *ean* and *philo* come together, it means *if I love with a genuine love* or *if I really love them.*

If Jesus really loves His Church — *and He does* — He takes action and gets involved when it is in trouble. He doesn't sit on the sidelines and watch His people continue in pride and disobedience. His actions are proof of His sincere love.

Out of Genuine Love, Jesus 'Rebukes' and 'Chastens'

One specific way Jesus said He proves His love for us is to "rebuke" us. The phrase "I rebuke" in Greek is *elegcho*, and it means *to expose, convict, or cross-examine for the purpose of conviction, as when convicting a lawbreaker in a court of law.* The word *elegcho* can also describe *a lawyer who brings evidence that is indisputable and undeniable, so the accused person's actions are irrefutably brought to light and the offender is exposed and convicted.*

In a positive sense this word is used *to convince someone of something.* It denotes *a lawyer who worked diligently to convince people of a new way of thinking or a new way of seeing things.* Interestingly, the word *elegcho* is the same word used in John 16:8 to describe the convicting ministry of the Holy Spirit. When He convicts us, He not only reveals what is wrong, He also works diligently to convince us of a new way of thinking and a new way of seeing things. Thus, a better translation for the phrase "I rebuke" would be "I convict and convince."

That is what Jesus was doing with the church of Laodicea. He convicted them of their condition, saying they were wretched, miserable, poor, blind, and naked. Then He immediately began to convince them of a new way to think and see things, and urged them to buy gold tried in the fire and white raiment to clothe their shame.

Not only did Jesus say "I rebuke," He also said "[I] chasten." The phrase "[I] chasten" is the Greek word *paideuo*, which means *I teach* or *I train.* It carries the idea of *training a child, or anyone, with discipline to help them mature and become a responsible adult.* Moreover it means *to assist one in reaching his or her full potential.* In Jesus' dealings with the church of Laodicea, He didn't just point out their faults and leave them to figure things out on their own. He came alongside them to educate and teach them and do everything in His power to help the believers turn from error and get back on track to spiritual maturity.

Our Response Is To 'Repent'

There is only one response to Jesus' correction, and that is to "…be zealous therefore, and repent" (Revelation 3:19). The phrase "be zealous" is a translation of the Greek word *zeloo*, which means *to be heated or to boil.* It denotes *enthusiasm, fervor, passion, devotion, or an eagerness to achieve something.* It carries *the idea of being deeply committed to something — even to be moved with envy, hatred, or anger.* By using this word, Jesus is telling us to be deeply moved and heated — even angry — over the condition which He is convicting us. And to let that emotion energize us to truly repent and change.

The word "repent" in verse 19 is the Greek word *metanoeo*, and it means *a change of mind that results in a complete, radical, total change of behavior; a* decision to completely change or to entirely turn around in the way that one is thinking, believing, or living. This describes a total transformation affecting every part of a person's life, both inside and outside, resulting in a behavioral change. Repentance has nothing to do with emotions; it is a decision of the will to turn from sin and toward God.

Jesus gave the order to "repent" — the Greek word *metanoeo* — five times in Revelation 2 and 3. He told the church of Ephesus to repent (Revelation 2:5); the church of Pergamum to repent (Revelation 2:16); the church of Thyatira to repent (Revelation 2:21, 22); the church of Sardis to repent (Revelation 3:3); and the church of Laodicea to repent (Revelation 3:19). Today, Jesus is still telling His Church to repent — to make *a decision of the will* and turn from sin and toward Him.

STUDY QUESTIONS

Study to shew thyself approved unto God, a workman that needeth not to be ashamed, rightly dividing the word of truth.
— 2 Timothy 2:15

When Jesus spoke to the church of Laodicea, He brought them discipline. Although no one likes it, discipline is a vital ingredient to our spiritual maturity. Carefully reflect on what God says about discipline in Hebrews 12:5-11 (also consider Proverbs 10:17; 12:1; 15:5).

1. Why should you *embrace* and not despise (hate) God's discipline? What is it a clear sign of?
2. As you respectfully receive God's discipline, what blessings can you expect to receive?

PRACTICAL APPLICATION

But be ye doers of the word, and not hearers only,
deceiving your own selves.
— James 1:22

1. When was the last time you experienced God's correction and discipline? What kind of thinking or behavior was He trying to correct? Did you repent?
2. Is God trying to correct and discipline you right now? If so, what is it regarding? What *new way of thinking or new way of seeing things* is He

trying to convince you? What steps can you take to better cooperate with His correction?

3. The best thing you can do when God corrects you is to *repent*. Along with conviction, His Holy Spirit brings *godly sorrow* that leads us to repentance. In your own words, describe what true repentance looks like. (As you answer, consider Second Corinthians 7:9,10; Joel 2:12-14; First John 1:9.)

TOPIC

Christ Pounding at the Door of the Church

SCRIPTURE

1. **Revelation 3:14-20** —And unto the angel of the church of the Laodiceans write; These things saith the Amen, the faithful and true witness, the beginning of the creation of God; I know thy works, that thou art neither cold nor hot: I would thou wert cold or hot. So then because thou art lukewarm, and neither cold nor hot, I will spue thee out of my mouth. Because thou sayest, I am rich, and increased with goods, and have need of nothing; and knowest not that thou art wretched, and miserable, and poor, and blind, and naked: I counsel thee to buy of me gold tried in the fire, that thou mayest be rich; and white raiment, that thou mayest be clothed, and that the shame of thy nakedness do not appear; and anoint thine eyes with eyesalve, that thou mayest see. [I] as many as [if] I love, I rebuke and [I] chasten: be zealous therefore, and repent. Behold, I stand at the door, and knock: if any man hear my voice, and open the door, I will come in to him, and will sup with him, and he with me.

GREEK WORDS

1. "I" — ἐγὼ (*ego*): He used this word repeatedly to draw attention to Himself

2. "if I love" — ἐὰν ἐγὼ φιλῶ (*ean ego philo*): the word ἐὰν (*ean*) means "if" and states how Christ deals with those He loves; the word φιλῶ (*philo*) is from φιλέω (*phileo*) and depicts affection, fondness, or real love; together, "if I love with a genuine love"

3. "I rebuke" — ἐλέγχω (*elegcho*): I rebuke; to expose, convict, or cross-examine for the purpose of conviction, as when convicting a lawbreaker in a court of law; a lawyer who brings evidence that is indisputable and undeniable, so the accused person's actions are irrefutably brought to light and the offender is exposed and convicted; used in a positive sense to convince someone of something; denotes a lawyer who worked diligently to convince people of a new way of thinking or a new way of seeing things

4. "I chasten" — παιδεύω (*paideuo*): I teach and train; to train children, or anyone, with strict discipline to help them mature and become responsible adults; to assist one in reaching full potential

5. "be zealous" — ζηλόω (*zeloo*): to be heated or to boil; enthusiasm, fervor, passion, devotion, or an eagerness to achieve something; to be deeply committed to something; even to be moved with envy, hatred, anger

6. "therefore" — οὖν (*oun*): consequently

7. "repent" — μετανοέω (*metanoeo*): a change of mind that results in a complete, radical, total change of behavior; a decision to completely change or to entirely turn around in the way that one is thinking, believing, or living; to entirely turn around; a total transformation affecting every part of a person's life, both inside and outside, resulting in a behavioral change

8. "Behold" — ἰδού (*idou*): bewilderment, shock, amazement, and wonder

9. "I stand" — ἵστημι (*histemi*): I stand; I stand by; I stand in the midst

10. "at" — ἐπί (*epi*): upon; at; right at; right there, right now

11. "the door" — τὴν θύραν (*ten thuran*): not just a door, but THE door; the word θύρα (*thura*) pictures a large and solid door; such doors were usually locked with a heavy bolt that slid through rings attached to the door and the frame; when such doors were opened, it provided access that was normally restricted; hence, it denotes an opportunity

12. "knock" — κρούω (*krouo*): to knock; the tense means to incessantly beat on a door; nonstop pounding; to implore one to open the door by nonstop knocking and pounding

13. "if" — ἐάν (*ean*): means "if," and states that Christ is making an offer to any who will respond

14. "any man" — τις (*tis*): anyone; gender is neutral; any man, any woman; in this case, if anyone in the Church or anyone who hears My pounding

15. "hear" — ἀκούω (*akouo*): hear or perceive; to comprehend by hearing; where we get the word "acoustic"

16. "voice" — φωνή (*phone*): voice; the sounds of words; this tells us how Christ pounds on the door; it is by His voice speaking to us

17. "open" — ἀνοίγω (*anoigo*): to make way, to give entrance; to throw wide open; pictures a grand and magnificent opening

SYNOPSIS

By the end of the First Century, a Christian church had been planted and was thriving in the opulent city of Laodicea. It is believed that Epaphras, an associate of the apostle Paul from the city of Colossae, started the church years earlier around the same time he planted churches in the cities of Hierapolis and Colossae.

Apparently, Laodicea's wealth was just as prevalent among the members of its church as it was in the rest of the city. In fact, they were doing so well that their passionate pursuit of knowing Christ was eventually replaced by religious ritual. By the time we come to Revelation 3:20, Jesus had been thrust from the church and was on the outside trying to get back in. To be clear, the Laodiceans were good people doing good things, but their riches had blinded them to their deplorable spiritual condition, and Jesus was greatly grieved.

The emphasis of this lesson:

Just as the Laodicean believers had pushed Jesus out of the church, there are churches and believers today who have done similarly. Still, He stands at the door and incessantly knocks, waiting to be given entrance. Those who open the door give Him opportunity to work in their lives.

Christ began His message to the church of Laodicea in Revelation 3:14 by saying, "And unto the angel of the church of the Laodiceans write; These things saith the Amen, the faithful and true witness, the beginning of the creation of God." Here we see one of the names Jesus gave to

Himself is "the Amen." In Greek, there is a definite article preceding the word "Amen," which indicates that Jesus is not just *an* amen — He is *THE Amen*. That is, He is THE FINAL WORD and has the final say-so regarding everything in your life. Regardless of what you're facing, no demon in hell and no man on earth has the final word. Only Christ Himself is THE Amen in your life!

As the church in Laodicea basked in their abundance, they developed an attitude of pride and self-reliance. Jesus personally observed this and began to confront them head-on. He told them, "I know thy works, that thou art neither cold nor hot: I would thou wert cold or hot. So then because thou art lukewarm, and neither cold nor hot, I will spue thee out of my mouth" (Revelation 3:15,16). These verses are packed with meaning, which we covered in Lessons 2, 3, and 4. Please refer back to these lessons to refresh and deepen your understanding of what we learned.

What Was the Church of Laodicea Saying About Itself?

When we come to Revelation 3:17, we hear Jesus exposing the error of the Laodicean believers. He said, "Because thou sayest, I am rich, and increased with goods, and have need of nothing; and knowest not that thou art wretched, and miserable, and poor, and blind, and naked."

The arrogance of the Laodiceans is seen from the first three words they spoke: "I am rich." The words "I am" in Greek is the word *eimi*, and it points to *self-reliance, self-absorption,* and *self-embellishment*. The word "rich" is the Greek word *Plousios*, which describes *wealth so great it cannot be tabulated*. Here it is capitalized, which is rare. It indicates that the Laodiceans were saying they were *The Richest* of all the churches and no one was more affluent than them.

They also said they were "increased with goods," which in Greek means *rich and endowed with resources*. In context here, it is the equivalent of saying, "I have made myself rich; I have resourced myself." These believers were so conceited and self-sufficient they said they had "...need of nothing." This phrase is a translation of the Greek words *ouden cheiran*. The word *ouden* means *absolutely nothing*, and the word *cheiran* depicts *a need or deficit*. When these words are joined, it means *absolutely no need of anything whatsoever*.

Jesus Set the Record Straight
About Their True Condition

In His candid, cut-to-the-chase way, Jesus pulled back the curtain of deception and revealed the Laodicean believers' true spiritual condition. He said, "...and knowest not that thou art wretched, and miserable, and poor, and blind, and naked" (Revelation 3:17).

"Knowest not" in Greek is *ouk oidas*. The word *ouk* means *emphatically not*, and the word *oidas* is from *oida*, which means *to see, perceive, understand*, or *comprehend*. Compounded, the words *ouk oidas* indicate *a total lack of comprehension*. It is the same as Jesus saying, "You emphatically do not see, perceive, understand, or comprehend your real spiritual condition."

He then proceeded to reveal that the Laodicean church was "...wretched, and poor, and blind, and naked." In Greek, the word "wretched" is *ho talaiporos*. The word *talaiporos* means *calloused* or *in a calloused condition*, and because the definitive article *ho* is coupled with *talaiporos*, it indicates that the Laodicean church was *THE most miserable and calloused of everyone*. It is no wonder they were also poor, blind, and naked.

He Counseled Them and Said To 'Anoint Their Eyes'

In Revelation 3:18, Jesus offered His wisdom and assistance to the Laodiceans. He said, "I counsel thee to buy of me gold tried in the fire, that thou mayest be rich; and white raiment, that thou mayest be clothed...." We have seen that the words "I counsel" in Greek is *sumbouleuo*, which describes *a joint decision to take action*. Thus, when Jesus said "I counsel thee," He was essentially saying, "Hey, let's you and Me get together and make a decision on how to fix this situation." Without question, He is willing to come to the bargaining table and work things out with anyone who is willing to do so.

In addition to buying gold tried in the fire and white raiment, Jesus told the Laodiceans, "...anoint thine eyes with eyesalve, that thou mayest see" (Revelations 3:18). This was a significant statement He made — one the Laodiceans could easily understand. Remember, there was a large medical school in their town renowned for its Phrygian eye medicine. The salve was a proven cure for sick eyes if it was applied correctly. When Jesus said they were to "anoint" their eyes with eye salve, He was saying "You need the anointing — *My anointing* — to touch your eyes that you may see."

The word "see" in Greek is the word *blepo*, which means *to see, behold, or to be aware*. This word is often intended to jolt and jar a listener or viewer to perk up and really listen to what is being said or to what is being seen. Hence, for the eyes of the Laodicean believers to be opened and their sight restored, they needed to come to Jesus — the Source of the anointing. He had everything they needed.

Jesus' Love for Us Moves Him To Action

In our last lesson, we focused on Revelation 3:19 which says, "As many as I love, I rebuke and chasten: be zealous therefore, and repent." In the original Greek text, there are a few words that do not appear in the English translation. The Greek actually says, "[I] as many as [if] I love, I rebuke and [I] chasten: be zealous therefore, and repent."

In Greek, this verse opens with the word "I," which is the Greek word *ego*, and it *emphatically draws attention to Jesus Himself*. It is the equivalent of Him saying, "*I* am now going to tell you how *I personally* deal with wayward churches and disobedient believers."

He said, "[I] as many as [if] I love…." The word "if," which only appears in the original Greek, is the word *ean*. And while it means *if*, its use is the same as Jesus saying, "*If* I love someone…" The phrase "I love" in Greek is *ean philo*. The word *philo* is from *phileo* and depicts *affection, fondness*, or *real love*. When *ean* and *philo* come together, it means *if I love with a genuine love* or *if I really love them*. The implication here is that "if" (*ean*) Jesus "loves" (*philo*) someone, this is how He deals with them.

Thus, if Jesus really loves His Church — *and He does* — He takes action and gets involved when it is in trouble. He doesn't sit on the sidelines and watch His people continue in pride and disobedience. His actions are proof of His sincere love.

He 'Rebukes' and 'Chastens' His Church

The Bible tells us in Revelation 3:19 that one of the major ways Jesus takes action and proves His love for us is by "rebuking" us. The words "I rebuke" in Greek is *elegcho*, and it means *to expose, convict, or cross-examine for the purpose of conviction, as when convicting a lawbreaker in a court of law*. It can also describe *a lawyer who brings evidence that is indisputable and undeniable, so the accused person's actions are irrefutably brought to light and the offender is exposed and convicted*.

In a positive sense, the word *elegcho* is the same word used in John 16:8 to describe the convicting ministry of the Holy Spirit. When He convicts us, He not only reveals what is wrong, He also works diligently *to convince us of a new way of thinking and a new way of seeing things.* Therefore, a better translation for the phrase "I rebuke" would be "I convict and also convince people to take right action."

In Laodicea, Jesus was convicting the church of their lukewarm condition. Like a prosecuting attorney He exposed the fact that they were wretched, miserable, poor, blind, and naked. At the same time, He immediately began convincing them of a new way of thinking and seeing things, urging them to buy gold tried in the fire and white raiment to clothe their shame.

Along with rebuking the Laodicean church, Jesus also "chastened" them. The word "chasten" is the Greek word *paideuo,* which means *to teach* or *to train,* and it carries the idea of *training a child, or anyone, with discipline to help them mature and become a responsible adult.* Moreover, it means *to assist one in reaching his or her full potential.* Jesus didn't just point out the faults of the Laodiceans and give up on them. He came alongside them to educate, teach, and do everything in His power to help them break free from their disobedience and get back on track to spiritual maturity. This is the same thing He does for you when you disobey and stray from the path of right living.

He Wants Us To Repent

Our response to Jesus' rebuke and chastening always begins with repentance. He told the church in Laodicea, "…be zealous therefore, and repent" (Revelation 3:19). The phrase "be zealous" is a translation of the Greek word *zeloo,* which means *to be heated or to boil.* It depicts *enthusiasm, fervor, passion, devotion, or an eagerness to achieve something.* It means *to be deeply committed to something — even to be moved with envy, hatred, or anger.* By using this word, Jesus was telling the Laodicean church — and us — that we must do our part to see change; and our part starts with repentance.

The word "repent" in verse 19 is the Greek word *metanoeo.* It is a compound of the word *meta,* which describes *a change or metamorphosis,* and a form of the word *nous,* which is the word for *the mind.* Thus, the word "repent" means *to change one's mind or make a decision that results in a complete, radical, total change of behavior.* It denotes *a decision to completely change or to entirely turn around in the way that one is thinking, believing, or living.* It describes *a total transformation affecting every part of a person's life, both inside and outside, resulting in a behavioral change.*

To five of the seven major churches in the Roman province of Asia, Jesus gave the order to "repent." He told the church of Ephesus, the church of Pergamum, the church of Thyatira, the church of Sardis, and the church of Laodicea to repent. Still today, Jesus is telling His Church to repent — to make *a decision of the will* and turn away from sin and toward God. Repentance has nothing to do with emotions; it is *a decision of the will.*

Christ Is Standing at the Door 'Knocking'

When we come to Revelation 3:20, we find Jesus in a very unique position. He says, "Behold, I stand at the door, and knock: if any man hear my voice, and open the door, I will come in to him, and will sup with him, and he with me." Although many evangelists and pastors have used this verse to call unbelievers to salvation in Christ, it is not directed to the lost. Jesus was actually speaking to His Church — people who were saved but merely going through the motions of religious routine. These believers had drifted so far from their devotion to Christ that they had pushed Him outside the Church.

The verse opens with the word "Behold," which is the Greek word *idou,* and it describes *bewilderment, shock, amazement, and wonder.* It is the equivalent of Jesus saying, "Wow! I am shocked and absolutely amazed that I have been ejected from My Church — I'm now on the outside trying to get back in."

Next, he says, "I stand at the door...." The words "I stand" in Greek is the word *histemi,* which means *I stand; I stand by; I stand in the midst.* The word "at" is the word *epi* in Greek. It means *upon; at; right at.* In this particular verse, it indicates being *right there, right now.* Jesus was *right there* in that moment standing by "the door."

In Greek, "the door" is *ten thuran.* Here again, we see a definite article attached to the word "door" — it is the Greek word *ten.* It means this is not just *a* door, but *THE door* of the Church. The word "door" is the Greek word *thura,* and it pictures *a large and solid door.* Such doors were usually locked with a heavy bolt that slid through rings attached to the door and the frame. When such doors were opened, it provided access that was normally restricted. Hence, it denotes *an opportunity.*

Stop and get the picture of what was happening. Jesus Christ, the Son of God, was standing right at the door of the church in Laodicea — but He was outside the church. In other words, the church was closed to the presence of Jesus. They had shut and bolted the door, not giving Him entrance or opportunity to enter and minister freely.

What was Jesus doing as He stood at the door? The Bible says He was *knocking*. While you may have imagined this to be a gentle knock on the door, it was not. The word "knock" is the Greek word *krouo*, which means *to beat or pound on a door*. The verb tense here indicates *incessant beating* or *nonstop pounding on a door*, imploring the one inside to open it up.

Will You Accept Jesus' Invitation?

Jesus then said, "...if any man hear my voice..." (Revelation 3:20). The word "if" is the Greek word *ean*, which means *if*, and states that Christ is making an offer to any who will respond. Specifically, He says if "any man," which is the Greek word *tis*, and it means *anyone*. This word is *gender neutral*, meaning *any man, any woman*. In this case it indicates *anyone in the Church* or *anyone who hears My pounding*.

The word "hear" in Greek is the word *akouo*, and it means *to hear or perceive; to comprehend by hearing*. It is where we get the word "acoustic." Thus, Jesus is saying, "If any man or any woman hears, perceives, or comprehends My voice." In Greek, the word "voice" is *phone*, and it means *voice* or *the sounds of words*. This is how we know when Jesus is knocking — we hear His *voice*. His *voice* is His knocking on the door.

The voice of Jesus is the voice of the Holy Spirit speaking to us through God's Word and speaking directly to our spirit. Again and again and again, He incessantly pounds and beats at the door of our hearts by speaking to us; and if any man or woman in His Church will open the door, He will enter.

The word "open" is the Greek word *anoigo*, which means *to make way, to give entrance; to throw wide open*. It pictures *a grand and magnificent opening*. "The door" is again the Greek word *ten thuran*, which describes *the door of the church* or *the door of a person's life*. This word creates the picture of a large, heavy door that is bolted shut. When such doors were opened, they provided access that was normally restricted. Hence, "the door" denotes *a significant and weighty opportunity*.

Friend, Jesus is still speaking this message to His Church today. Sadly, many congregations and individuals have closed and bolted the door of their hearts, restricting His access and opportunity to work in their lives. Even now He is standing right at the door of *your* life, desiring to come in. The fact that you are reading this lesson at this moment is no accident. It is proof that Jesus is right there giving you a chance to open up and let His loving presence into your life. Will you open the door?

STUDY QUESTIONS

Study to shew thyself approved unto God, a workman that needeth not to be ashamed, rightly dividing the word of truth.
— 2 Timothy 2:15

1. Why do you think Jesus is always knocking at the door of your heart? What is His motivation for pursuing you? As you answer, take another look at Revelation 3:20.

2. The church of Laodicea was not the only one to push Jesus away—Nazareth, His own hometown, did the same thing. Carefully read Mark 6:1-6 (Matthew 13:53-58). How did the people of Nazareth close the door on Jesus? What was the result of their actions?

PRACTICAL APPLICATION

But be ye doers of the word, and not hearers only, deceiving your own selves.
— James 1:22

1. Christ's words in Revelation 3:20 to the church in Laodicea are not directed to the lost, but to *believers* who have drifted away from their passionate pursuit of Him. Does this describe you? Is your love for Jesus still on fire? What does Jesus' "knock" sound like in your life?

2. What does it look like to "push" Jesus outside the church, or outside one's life? Have you seen this happen in a church or to a friend? What changes did they subtly begin to make that pushed Jesus away? What have you learned *not* to do from their example?

3. Jesus stands at the door of *your* life every day desiring to come in. He is constantly knocking, waiting expectantly for you to open up and let Him make His presence and power real in your life. Will you open the door? If you're ready, we'd be honored to pray with you. Just give

us a call (1-800-742-5593), and we will join our faith with yours, praying for a fresh start in your life.

TOPIC
A Promise of Instant Intimacy for Those Who Open the Door

SCRIPTURE

1. **Revelation 3:14-20** — And unto the angel of the church of the Laodiceans write; These things saith the Amen, the faithful and true witness, the beginning of the creation of God; I know thy works, that thou art neither cold nor hot: I would thou wert cold or hot. So then because thou art lukewarm, and neither cold nor hot, I will spue thee out of my mouth. Because thou sayest, I am rich, and increased with goods, and have need of nothing; and knowest not that thou art wretched, and miserable, and poor, and blind, and naked. I counsel thee to buy of me gold tried in the fire, that thou mayest be rich; and white raiment, that thou mayest be clothed, and that the shame of thy nakedness do not appear; and anoint thine eyes with eyesalve, that thou mayest see. [I] as many as [if] I love, I rebuke and [I] chasten: be zealous therefore, and repent. Behold, I stand at the door, and knock: if any man hear my voice, and open the door, I will come in to him, and will sup with him, and he with me.

GREEK WORDS

1. "I" — ἐγὼ (*ego*): He used this word repeatedly to draw attention to Himself

2. "if I love" — ἐὰν ἐγὼ φιλῶ (*ean ego philo*): the word ἐὰ⊠ (ean) means "if" and states this is how Christ deals with those He loves; the word φιλῶ (*philo*) is from φιλέω (*phileo*) and depicts affection, fondness, or real love; together, "if I love with a genuine love"

3. "I rebuke" — ἐλέγχω (*elegcho*): to expose, convict, or cross-examine for the purpose of conviction as when convicting a lawbreaker in a court

of law; pictures a lawyer who brings evidence that is indisputable and undeniable, so the accused person's actions are irrefutably brought to light and the offender is exposed and convicted; used in a positive sense to convince someone of something; denotes a lawyer who worked diligently to convince people of a new way of thinking or a new way of seeing things

4. "I chasten" — **παιδεύω** (*paideuo*): I teach and train; to train children, or anyone, with strict discipline to help them mature and become responsible adults; to assist one in reaching full potential

5. "be zealous" — **ζηλόω** (*zeloo*): to be heated or to boil; enthusiasm, fervor, passion, devotion, or an eagerness to achieve something; to be deeply committed to something; even to be moved with envy, hatred, or anger

6. "therefore" — **οὖν** (*oun*): consequently

7. "repent" — **μετανοέω** (*metanoeo*): a change of mind that results in a complete, radical, total change of behavior; a decision to completely change or to entirely turn around in the way that one is thinking, believing, or living; to entirely turn around; a total transformation affecting every part of a person's life, both inside and outside, resulting in a behavioral change

8. "Behold" — **ἰδού** (*idou*): bewilderment, shock, amazement, and wonder

9. "I stand" — **ἵστημι** (*histemi*): I stand; I stand by

10. "at" — **ἐπί** (*epi*): upon; at; right at; right there, right now

11. "the door" — **τὴν θύραν** (*ten thuran*): definite article means not just a door, but THE door; the word **θύρα** (*thura*) pictures a large and solid door; such doors were usually locked with a heavy bolt that slid through rings attached to the door and the frame; when such doors were opened, it provided access that was normally restricted; hence, it denotes an opportunity

12. "knock" — **κρούω** (*krouo*): to knock; the tense means to incessantly beat on a door; nonstop pounding; to implore one to open the door by nonstop knocking and pounding

13. "if" — **ἐάν** (*ean*): means "if" and states that Christ is making an offer to any who will respond

14. "any man" — **τις** (*tis*): anyone; gender is neutral; any man, any woman; in this case, if anyone in the Church or anyone who hears My pounding

15. "hear" — **ἀκούω** (*akouo*): hear or perceive; to comprehend by hearing; where we get the word acoustic

16. "voice" — **φωνή** (*phone*): voice; the sounds of words; this tells us how Christ pounds on the door; it is by His voice speaking to us

17. "open" — **ἀνοίγω** (*anoigo*): to make way, to give entrance; to throw wide open; pictures a grand and magnificent opening

18. "I will come" — **εἰσέρχομαι** (*eiserchomai*): the form used means I will immediately enter; I will quickly come right into; depicts seizing the opportunity to make a quick entrance

19. "to" — **πρός** (*pros*): toward; headed in a direction toward

20. "sup" — **δειπνέω** (*deipneo*): dinner; a later afternoon or evening dinner; such dinners were reserved only for the closest of companions and friends; the use of this word tells us that Christ will enter into companionship, friendship, and intimacy with anyone who responds to His voice

21. "with" — **μετ'** (*met'*): depicts companionship or close association; to do something in conjunction with someone else; partnership

SYNOPSIS

If you travel to the site of the ancient city of Laodicea today, you will see the remnants of a town that have reemerged from the earth in the last decade. Archaeologists have worked vigorously and gone to great lengths to excavate this fabulously lavish metropolis and have succeeded in their endeavors.

History reveals that by the end of the First Century, there was a church in Laodicea, and it was one of the seven major churches in the Roman province of Asia. In fact, it was the last church Christ addressed in the book of Revelation.

In Revelation 3:20, Jesus said, "Behold, I stand at the door, and knock: if any man hear my voice, and open the door, I will come in to him, and will sup with him, and he with me." Somehow, in the midst of all the church's pursuits, Jesus had been pushed outside of the church. Christian life had become very routine, and well-meaning believers were no longer including the Lord in their spiritual activities. Sadly, this same dilemma is still entrapping many churches and believers today. Nevertheless, Jesus continues to stand at the door and knock — wanting and waiting to be readmitted.

The emphasis of this lesson:

For those who choose to hear Jesus' voice and open the door to Him, He will immediately respond. Rich, intimate companionship and partnership is reserved for any church or individual who welcomes Him and gives Him the opportunity to work in their lives.

Let's quickly review the first verses of Christ's message to the church of Laodicea, highlighting once more some important insights we have discovered throughout our study. Jesus began in verse 14 saying:

> **And unto the angel of the church of the Laodiceans write; These things saith the Amen, the faithful and true witness, the beginning of the creation of God (Revelation 3:14).**

We noted in Lesson 1 that Jesus declared Himself to be "...the beginning of the creation of God." In Greek, "the beginning" is *he arche*. The word *arche* describes *the initial starting point; what comes first and is hence chief above all; highest in priority; preeminent*. Because the definite article *he* is included, it means that Jesus is not *a* beginning — He is absolutely "THE very beginning of all things." He is the Originator and the Creator of the creation of God. Christ went on to say:

> **I know thy works, that thou art neither cold nor hot: I would thou wert cold or hot. So then because thou art lukewarm, and neither cold nor hot, I will spue thee out of my mouth (Revelation 3:15,16).**

We saw in Lessons 2 and 3 that the words "I know" is the Greek word *oida*, which means *to see, perceive, understand, or comprehend*; it pictures *knowledge gained by personal experience or personal observation*. Jesus had been personally observing the church of Laodicea — from the outside — and had seen all their activities, actions, and deeds. Now He was going to present them with a factual report of His investigation. He began by stating:

> **Because thou sayest, I am rich, and increased with goods, and have need of nothing; and knowest not that thou art wretched, and miserable, and poor, and blind, and naked (Revelation 3:17).**

Jesus had personally observed and was well-acquainted with all seven of the churches He addressed in the book of Revelation. All of them had reputations — in their own eyes and in the eyes of society. Yet what Jesus saw often did not match what they saw. The church of Ephesus for example, had a reputation for being the biggest and greatest church of all. In most people's minds, no one was greater than Ephesus. But when Jesus addressed them in Revelation 2:5, He told them to repent because they had left their first love — they had completely fallen from the place of intimacy they once had with Him.

Then there was the church of Sardis. The Bible says they had a "name," or reputation, for being "alive." However when Jesus carefully looked them over, He said they were *dead* (*see* Revelation 3:1). He saw something different than what everyone else was seeing.

The same was true of the church of Laodicea. They bragged saying, "I am rich." The word for "rich" in Greek is *Plousios*, which describes *extravagant wealth that cannot be counted*. And because the word *Plousios* is capitalized in the Greek, it indicates that the Laodiceans were claiming to be *THE richest of all*. Yet when Jesus personally observed them, He saw something quite the contrary.

He told them they were "wretched," which in Greek is *ho talaiporos*. The word *talaiporos* means *calloused; negatively affected*; or *in a calloused condition*. The fact that a definite article — the word *ho* — is tacked on in front indicates the Laodicean church was *THE most calloused of everyone*. Jesus had been trying to speak to them, but their calloused hearts prevented them from hearing His voice.

He went on to say they were "miserable" — the Greek word *eleeinos*, which means *to be pitied*. In addition, Jesus said these believers were also "poor," which in Greek is the word *ptochos*, describing *the lowest category of all poor people*. Furthermore, He said they were "blind" and "naked." The word "blind" is the word *tuphlos*, and it depicts *a person who has been intentionally blinded by someone else; one whose eyes have been deliberately removed or gouged out so that he is blinded*. This person hasn't just lost his sight, but he no longer has eyes to see the truth. In this case, the believers in Laodicea couldn't see that they were spiritually "naked," which in Greek is the word *gumnos*, and it means *completely naked*. To recover from their deplorable condition, Jesus said:

> **I counsel thee to buy of me gold tried in the fire, that thou mayest be rich; and white raiment, that thou mayest be clothed,**

and that the shame of thy nakedness do not appear; and anoint thine eyes with eyesalve, that thou mayest see (Revelation 3:18).

In Lesson 5, we learned that the phrase "I counsel" in Greek is the word *sumbouleuo*, which is from the words *sun* and *bouleuo*. The word *sun* means "together" and carries the idea of *an association* or *doing something jointly with someone else*. The word *bouleuo* means *to advise, counsel, or determine*. When compounded, the word *sumbouleuo* pictures *a joint counseling or a joint determination*. Thus, the phrase "I counsel" is the equivalent of Jesus appealing to the church in Laodicea and saying, "Hey, let's you and Me come together and make a decision on how to fix things and determine to get it done."

We also see from this verse that Christ wants us to be spiritually enriched and "clothed" in white raiment. The word "clothed" is the Greek word *periballo*, and it means *enrobed* or *having garments wrapped around a person*. When we are clothed with the dazzling and resplendent garments of Jesus' righteousness, the shame of our nakedness does not appear.

"Shame" in Greek is the word *aischune*, and it describes *disgrace, embarrassment, or humiliation*. And the phrase "not appear" in Greek means *will not become visibly evident*. Jesus always seeks to preserve our dignity — He has no desire whatsoever to embarrass or humiliate us. Essentially what He is saying here is, "I don't want anyone to see your debased condition. I want it to be covered by the robe of righteousness I've made available to you."

Jesus then said, "…anoint thine eyes with eyesalve, that thou mayest see." Remember, Jesus had revealed to the Laodicean church that they were blind to their true spiritual state. He offered them His anointing, and if they would humbly receive it and apply it to their eyes, their spiritual sight would be restored. The word "see" in Greek is *blepo*, which means *to see, behold, or to be aware*. It was often used to jolt and jar a listener or viewer to perk up and really listen to what was being said or to what was being seen. Like the Laodicean believers, you too may need Jesus' anointing to open your eyes. If so, simply come to Him and ask for it. He is the Source of everything you need!

[I] as many as [if] I love, I rebuke and [I] chasten: be zealous therefore, and repent (Revelation 3:19).

Notice the first word "I." It only appears in the Greek text, and it is the Greek word *ego*. The use of this word *emphatically draws attention to Jesus*

Himself. It is the equivalent of Jesus saying, "*I* am now going to tell you how *I* personally deal with people who need correction."

Next, note the phrase "[if] I love." In Greek it is *ean ego philo.* The word *ean* means *if* and states how Christ deals with those He loves; the word *ego* is *I*, and the word *philo* is from *phileo*, which depicts *affection, fondness,* or *real love.* When *ean ego philo* come together, it means *if I love with a genuine love* or *if I really love them.* Like a good parent who truly loves their child, Jesus said, "If I really, genuinely love you, then I'm going to rebuke and chasten you."

The word "rebuke" in Greek is *elegcho*, and it means *to expose, convict, or cross-examine for the purpose of conviction, as when a lawbreaker is convicted in a court of law.* The word *elegcho* can also describe *a lawyer who brings evidence that is indisputable and undeniable, so the accused person's actions are irrefutably brought to light and the offender is exposed and convicted.*

In a positive sense, this word describes *convincing someone of something. For instance,* it denotes *a lawyer who worked diligently to convince people of a new way of thinking or a new way of seeing things.* Interestingly, the word *elegcho* is the same word used in John 16:8 to describe the convicting ministry of the Holy Spirit. When we've done something wrong, the Holy Spirit brings it to our attention — He presents irrefutable evidence of how we have erred. At the same time, He also works diligently to convince us of a new way of thinking and a new way of seeing things. He shows us what actions we need to take to self-correct. This is exactly what Jesus did with the church of Laodicea.

The Bible also says that He "chastened" them. The word "chasten" in Greek is *paideuo*, and it means *to teach* or *to train* — like *the teaching and training of a child with strict discipline to help him mature and become a responsible adult.* The word *paideuo* also describes *assisting one in reaching his or her full potential.* When Jesus dealt with the church of Laodicea, He didn't just tell them what they did wrong. He also educated them and did everything in His power to help them turn from error and get back on track to spiritual maturity.

Along with Jesus' rebuke and chastening, He urged the Laodicean believers to "…be zealous therefore, and repent" (Revelation 3:19). The phrase "be zealous" is a translation of the Greek word *zeloo*, which means *to be heated or to boil.* It denotes *enthusiasm, fervor, passion, devotion, and a deep commitment to achieve something — even to be moved with envy, hatred, or anger.* Thus, when Jesus said, "Be zealous," He was telling the Laodiceans, "Let your anger and frustration over what I've revealed to you about your spiritual condition move you to take action to see things change."

The first action we're to take when convicted of sin is to "repent." Although there is much confusion on this subject today, repentance was taught by Jesus, John the Baptist, the apostle Peter, and the apostle Paul all through the New Testament. The word "repent" — the Greek word *metanoeo* — is a compound of the word *meta*, which means *change*, and *noeo*, a form of the word *nous*, which describes *the mind*. Hence, repentance is *a change of mind that results in a complete, radical, total change of behavior; a decision to completely change or to entirely turn around in the way that one is thinking, believing, or living*. Repentance is *a decision of the will* to turn from sin and toward God — emotions are not involved.

> **Behold, I stand at the door, and knock: if any man hear my voice, and open the door, I will come in to him, and will sup with him, and he with me (Revelation 3:20).**

Where was Jesus when He was saying all these things? Revelation 3:20 tells us He was *outside of the church*. This verse opens with the word "Behold," which is the Greek word *idou*, and it describes *bewilderment, shock, amazement, and wonder*. It is the equivalent of Jesus saying, "Wow! I'm shocked and amazed that I've been evicted from My church — I'm on the outside trying to get back in."

Next, He said, "I stand at the door...." The words "I stand" in Greek is the word *histemi*, which means *I stand; I stand by; I stand in the midst*. The word "at" is the word *epi* in Greek. It means *upon; at;* or *right at*. Here, it indicates that Jesus was *right there* in that moment standing by "the door."

In Greek, "the door" is *ten thuran*. It includes a definite article, which means this is not just *a* door, but *THE door* of the Church. The word "door" is the Greek word *thura*, and it pictures *a large and solid door*. Such doors were usually locked with a heavy bolt that slid through rings attached to the door and the frame. When such doors were opened, it provided access that was normally restricted. Hence, this "door" denotes *an opportunity*.

What was Jesus doing as He stood at the door? The Bible says He was "knocking." The word "knock" is the Greek word *krouo*, which means *to beat or pound on a door.* The verb tense here indicates *incessant beating* or *nonstop pounding on a door*, imploring the one inside to open up.

Jesus then said, "…If any man hear my voice…" (Revelation 3:20). The phrase "any man" is the Greek word *tis*, and it means *anyone*. This word is *gender neutral* and indicates *any man* or *any woman in the Church* or *anyone who hears My pounding.*

The word "hear" in Greek is the word *akouo*, and it means *to hear or perceive; to comprehend by hearing*. It is from where we get the word "acoustics." Hence, Jesus said, "If any man or any woman hears, perceives, or comprehends My voice and opens the door, I will come in to him, and will sup with him, and he with Me."

The word "open" is the Greek word *anoigo*, and it means *to make way, to give entrance; to throw wide open*. It pictures *a grand and magnificent opening*. "The door" is again the Greek phrase *ten thuran*, and it describes *the door of the church* or *the door of a person's life that has been slammed or bolted shut*. When such a door is opened, it provides access and opportunities that are normally restricted. Therefore, when Jesus said, "…If any man hear my voice, and open the door, I will come in to him," He is saying, "Whoever will just crack the door and give Me an opportunity, I will immediately seize it."

Then He said, "…and [I] will sup with him, and he with me." The word "sup" in Greek is *deipneo*, and it describes *a later afternoon or evening dinner*. Such dinners were *full banquets reserved only for the closest of companions and friends*. The use of this word tells us that *Christ will quickly enter into companionship, friendship, and intimacy with anyone who responds to His voice*. Remember, His "voice" — the Greek word *phone*, which describes *the sounds of words* — is His knocking.

Finally, did you notice the way Jesus described the dinner setting in verse 20? He said, "[I] with him, and he with me." The word "with," which appears twice, is the same Greek word in both places — the word *met*. Why is this significant? Because the word *met* depicts *companionship or close association*; it pictures *doing something in conjunction with someone else; partnership*.

Listen… Can you hear Jesus calling? His voice is His knock at the door of your heart. He stands, ready, willing, and able to enter into your life and heal the hurts, bind up the broken places, and share a close companionship and partnership with you — the likes of which cannot be fully put into words. If you'll crack open the door to your heart, He will most certainly come in!

STUDY QUESTIONS

Study to shew thyself approved unto God, a workman that needeth not to be ashamed, rightly dividing the word of truth.
— 2 Timothy 2:15

1. In Revelation 3:20, Jesus offers a priceless invitation of intimate companionship to any man or woman who *hears His voice* and opens the door. In this verse, Jesus is letting you know that *you can hear His voice.* Take a few moments to reflect on these promises from God's Word. What insights about hearing God's voice is He showing you in these passages?
    *   **John 10:4,5,27**
    *   **Isaiah 30:21**
    *   **Isaiah 50:4,5; Proverbs 8:32-35**
    *   **Psalm 25:9,12; 32:8**
    *   **Jeremiah 33:3**
    *   **John 16:12-15**

PRACTICAL APPLICATION

But be ye doers of the word, and not hearers only, deceiving your own selves.
— James 1:22

Augustine said, "To fall in love with God is the greatest of all romances; to seek Him, the greatest adventure; to find Him, the greatest human achievement." The Holy Spirit — who is the Spirit of Christ — stands at the door of your heart daily and knocks. He longs for you to welcome Him and include Him in every part of your life!

1. According to Scripture, what are some of the blessings of being intimately connected in relationship with Jesus? (*See* Psalm 25:14; Amos 3:7; John 15:15; First Corinthians 2:9,10.)

2. What benefits and blessings have you personally enjoyed as you've been in relationship with Jesus? What things are you most grateful for?

3. When life gets busy and your personal time with God gets postponed for one or more days, what do you miss most about being with Him? Can your family members and close friends tell when you haven't spent time with Him? What are the telltale signs that give it away?

4. Name the top three things in your life that distract you or disrupt your intimate time with God. What practical steps can you take to limit or eliminate these things from robbing you of your time with Him?

LESSON 9

TOPIC

The Commitment To Constantly Be Overcoming

SCRIPTURE

1. **Revelation 3:14-22** — And unto the angel of the church of the Laodiceans write; These things saith the Amen, the faithful and true witness, the beginning of the creation of God; I know thy works, that thou art neither cold nor hot: I would thou wert cold or hot. So then because thou art lukewarm, and neither cold nor hot, I will spue thee out of my mouth. Because thou sayest, I am rich, and increased with goods, and have need of nothing; and knowest not that thou art wretched, and miserable, and poor, and blind, and naked: I counsel thee to buy of me gold tried in the fire, that thou mayest be rich; and white raiment, that thou mayest be clothed, and that the shame of thy nakedness do not appear; and anoint thine eyes with eyesalve, that thou mayest see. [I] as many as [if] I love, I rebuke and [I] chasten: be zealous therefore, and repent. Behold, I stand at the door, and knock: if any man hear my voice, and open the door, I will come in to him, and will sup with him, and he with me. To him that overcometh will I grant to sit with me in my throne, even as I also overcame, and am set

down with my Father in his throne. He that hath an ear, let him hear what the Spirit saith unto the churches.

GREEK WORDS

1. "Behold" — ἰδού (*idou*): bewilderment, shock, amazement, and wonder

2. "I stand" — ἵστημι (*histemi*): I stand; I stand by

3. "at" — ἐπί (*epi*): upon; at; right at; right there, right now

4. "the door" — τὴν θύραν (*ten thuran*): definite article means not just a door, but THE door; the word θύρα (*thura*) pictures a large and solid door; such doors were usually locked with a heavy bolt that slid through rings attached to the door and the frame; when such doors were opened, it provided access that was normally restricted; hence, it denotes an opportunity

5. "knock" — κρούω (*krouo*): to knock; the tense means to incessantly beat on a door; nonstop pounding; to implore one to open the door by his nonstop knocking and pounding

6. "if" — ἐάν (*ean*): means "if" and states that Christ is making an offer to any who will respond

7. "any man" — τις (*tis*): anyone; gender is neutral; any man, any woman; in this case, if anyone in the church or anyone who hears my pounding

8. "hear" — ἀκούω (*akouo*): hear or perceive; to comprehend by hearing;

9. "voice" — φωνή (*phone*): voice; the sounds of words; this tells us Christ pounds on the door by speaking to us

10. "open" — ἀνοίγω (*anoigo*): to make way, to give entrance; to throw wide open; pictures a grand and magnificent opening

11. "the door" — τὴν θύραν (*ten thuran*): definite article means not just a door, but THE door; the word θύρα (*thura*) pictures a large and solid door; such doors were usually locked with a heavy bolt that slid through rings attached to the door and the frame; when such doors were opened, it provided access that was normally restricted; hence, it denotes an opportunity

12. "I will come" — εἰσέρχομαι (*eiserchomai*): the form used means, "I will immediately enter" or, "I will quickly come right into"; depicts Jesus seizing the opportunity to make a quick entrance

13. "to" — πρός (*pros*): toward; headed in a direction toward

14. "sup" — δειπνέω (*deipneo*): dinner; a later afternoon or evening dinner; such dinners were reserved only for the closest of companions and friends; the use of this word tells that Christ will enter into companionship, friendship, and intimacy with anyone who responds to His voice

15. "with" — μετ' (*met'*): depicts companionship or close association; to do something in conjunction with someone else; partnership

16. "to him that overcometh" — ὁ νικῶν (*ho nikon*): the words ὁ νικῶν (*ho nikon*), literally, the one who is perpetually overcoming; the root word νικάω (*nikao*) describes an overcomer, conqueror, champion, victor, master, or an overwhelming, prevailing force; when compounded, it can be translated as more than conquerors, overwhelming conquerors, victors paramount, or enormous overcomers; this word is so power-packed that one could translate it as a phenomenal, walloping conquering force

17. "will I grant" — δώσω (*doso*): a future form of the Greek word *didomi*, which means "I give," but in this verse could mean "I allow" or, "I permit"

18. "to sit" — καθίζω (*kathidzo*): to sit; to sit down; anyone who responds to Christ will be invited immediately to sit with him in His throne; no delay, but immediately

19. "with" — μετ' ἐμοῦ (*met' emou*): with; depicts companionship or close association; to do something in conjunction with someone else; partnership

20. "in my throne" — ἐν τῷ θρόνῳ μου (*en to throno mou*): literally, "in the throne of Me"; word "throne" (θρόνος, *thronos*) denotes the seat or throne for the head of a country or nation; a king was the uncontested highest power of his country and there was no higher authority, no higher law, and no higher power than the king in his own realm; because he was endued with unmatched power and authority, he sat enthroned above all others

21. "even as I also" — ὡς κἀγὼ (*hos kago*): I also; me too

22. "overcame" — ἐνίκησα (*enikesa*): past tense of νικάω (*nikao*); describes an overcomer, conqueror, champion, victor, master, or an overwhelming, prevailing force; when compounded, it can be translated as more than conquerors, overwhelming conquerors, paramount victors, or enormous overcomers; this word is so power-packed that one could translate it as a phenomenal, walloping conquering force

23. "am set down" — **καθίζω** (*kathidzo*): am presently seated

24. "with" — **μετ᾽ ἐμοῦ** (*met' emou*): depicts companionship or close association; to do something in conjunction with someone else; partnership

SYNOPSIS

The message Jesus spoke to the church of Laodicea is a message He is still speaking to us today. The believers there had become so caught up in their religious routines that they were no longer including Him in their activities. In fact, they had pushed Him out of the church, and He was trying to get back in. Patiently, yet persistently, He stood at the church's door knocking — calling for someone to open the door. To anyone who would hear His voice and let Him in, He would immediately come in and reestablish intimate companionship. Furthermore, He said, "To him that overcometh will I grant to sit with me in my throne, even as I also overcame, and am set down with my Father in his throne" (Revelation 3:21).

The emphasis of this lesson:

Jesus has called His Church and all who are a part of it to be overcomers. We are wired for victory — not just one victory or a victory every now and then. We are called to perpetually overcome all obstacles that come our way. This is our destiny as followers of Christ.

A Brief Summary of Revelation 3:14-19

To the pastor and the people of the church in Laodicea living in the First Century, Jesus sent this message:

> **And unto the angel of the church of the Laodiceans write; These things saith the Amen, the faithful and true witness, the beginning of the creation of God. I know thy works, that thou art neither cold nor hot: I would thou wert cold or hot. So then because thou art lukewarm, and neither cold nor hot, I will spue thee out of my mouth (Revelation 3:14-16).**

After personally observing the actions and activities of this church, Jesus — the Faithful and True Witness — accurately assessed their spiritual condition and found them to be in trouble. They had lost the refreshing and revitalizing qualities they once had, leaving them in a stagnant state of mediocrity. Their attitude of indifference made Jesus so sick He was ready to vomit them out of His mouth.

As is often the case, pride was at the root of the Laodicean's halfhearted devotion. In Revelation 3:17, Jesus recalled the very words they had said about themselves: "Because thou sayest, I am rich, and increased with goods, and have need of nothing…." From their distorted perspective, they believed their level of success and material abundance had been achieved in their own strength. Contaminated by conceit, they boasted that they had absolutely no need of anything whatsoever — but nothing was further from the truth.

Motivated by loving compassion, Jesus candidly revealed to them that they were "…wretched, and miserable, and poor, and blind, and naked" (Revelation 3:17). One thing you can always count on Jesus to do is tell you the truth about yourself — as painful as it may be to hear. Still, if you will hear Him, receive what He says, and take the necessary steps to make things right, you'll be set free.

In response to the sick state of the Laodicean church, Jesus said, "I counsel thee to buy of me gold tried in the fire, that thou mayest be rich; and white raiment, that thou mayest be clothed, and that the shame of thy nakedness do not appear…" (Revelation 3:18). From the opening of Jesus' statement, He declares His commitment to His people. In Greek, the phrase "I counsel" is the equivalent of Him saying, "Let's come together on this and discover the best course of action, determining to carry it out until we see things change."

Clearly, the church of Laodicea was spiritually naked but oblivious to their condition. Jesus wanted to clothe them so the shame of their nakedness did not appear. This means He wanted to cover them in His righteousness so that the embarrassing and humiliating aspects of their lives would no longer be visible to others. He feels the same way about all believers, including you.

He then instructed the Laodiceans, "…anoint thine eyes with eyesalve, that thou mayest see" (Revelation 3:18). The word "anoint" here is Jesus' call for His people to take action — to seek Him for His anointing and apply it to their eyes so that their spiritual sight is restored. Pride had gouged out the eyes of the Laodiceans and made them blind to their true spiritual condition. Only the Holy Spirit can open blinded eyes and remove the scales of self-deception so that a person can truly "see" themselves and God accurately.

In Revelation 3:19, Jesus tells us clearly how He treats those He genuinely loves. The original Greek text records Him as saying, "[I] as many as [if] I love, I rebuke and [I] chasten: be zealous therefore, and repent." Because Jesus genuinely loved the church of Laodicea, He took the time to "rebuke them." This means He *convicted them of what they were doing wrong* and also *convinced them of a new way of thinking and seeing things*. He also "chastened" them, which means He took time *to teach and train* them with strict discipline to help them mature and reach their full potential. And because Jesus loves you, He will take the time to do the same in your life.

'Behold, I Stand at the Door and Knock'

When we come to Revelation 3:20, we find Jesus outside of the church trying to get back in. Astonished by His eviction, He said, "Behold, I stand at the door, and knock: if any man hear my voice, and open the door, I will come in to him, and will sup with him, and he with me." We have seen that the word "Behold" is the Greek word *idou*, and it reveals Jesus' *bewilderment, shock, amazement, and wonder*. Think of it: Jesus — the Head of the Church — was on the outside looking in. The people for whom He died and gave His life's Blood had banned Him from their lives and reassigned Him to the role of spectator. A mind-boggling situation indeed.

Nevertheless, Jesus said, "I stand at the door and knock...." The words "I stand" is the Greek word *histemi*, which means *I stand* or *I stand by*. The word "at" in Greek is the word *epi*, meaning *upon; at;* or *right at*. It carries the idea of *being right there, right now*. Jesus was *right there*, standing by "the door." In Greek, "the door" is *ten thuran*, which includes a definite article. This was not just *a* door; it was *THE door of the church*. It pictures *a large and solid door*; such doors were usually locked with a heavy bolt that slid through rings attached to the door and the frame. When such doors were opened, it provided access that was normally restricted. Hence, this door denotes an *opportunity*.

Jesus was stationed right in front of the door to the church in Laodicea, and He was *knocking*. In Greek, the word "knock" is the Greek word *krouo*, and it describes *nonstop pounding*. The tense here means *to incessantly beat on a door* or *to implore one to open the door by his nonstop knocking and pounding*. Jesus' love for His Church was what kept Him there knocking.

'If Any Man Hear My Voice'

Jesus went on to say, "…If any man hear my voice…" (Revelation 3:20). The word "if" in Greek is *ean*, which means *"if"* and indicates that Christ is making an offer to anyone who will respond. In fact, He says if "any man" hears His voice. The phrase "any man" is the Greek word *tis*, which means *anyone; the gender is neutral.* Thus, it is *any man, any woman,* or in this case, *if anyone in the church or anyone* who hears His voice.

The word "hear" is the Greek word *akouo*, which means *to hear or perceive; to comprehend by hearing.* And the word "voice" in Greek is *phone*, which means *voice* or *the sounds of words.* This tells us that Christ pounds on the door of our hearts by speaking to us. Most often, His voice comes to us in the form of His Word and directly through His Holy Spirit.

Consider this… God begins to deal with you about something out of line in your life. It could be any number of things; overeating and not taking care of your body, lying, gossiping, holding on to an offense, hanging out with the wrong crowd, or any kind of debilitating addiction. Again and again, the convicting voice of the Holy Spirit beats against the door of your heart, saying things like: "Change your attitude," "Choose to forgive and release them," "Tell the truth," "Be generous," "You don't need to go there," and the list goes on. Repeatedly He pounds with His words — cautioning, warning, redirecting, and imploring you to change. His voice will stay with you and continue to speak until you "open" the door and let Him.

The word "open" in Revelation 3:20 is the Greek word *anoigo*, which means *to make way, to give entrance; to throw wide open.* It pictures *a grand and magnificent opening* or *a crack in the doorway.* Every time you choose to hear Jesus' voice and obey, you open the door of your heart and give Him the opportunity to work in your life and take you into new levels of freedom.

'I Will Come in to Him and Sup with Him, and He with Me'

The moment the door is opened, Jesus said, "I will come." This phrase in Greek is the word *eiserchomai.* The form used here means, *"I will immediately enter"* or *"I will quickly come right into."* This word depicts Jesus seizing the opportunity to make a quick entrance. Even the word "to" is significant. It is the Greek word *pros*, and it means *toward; headed in a direction toward.* Basically, Jesus told the church in Laodicea, "If you just crack open the door, I will beeline-it into the church."

Once Jesus is inside, He said He would "sup" with us. "Sup" is the Greek word *deipneo*, and it describes *a later afternoon or evening dinner that was reserved only for the closest of companions and friends.* This meal was on the scale of a *banquet.* The use of this word tells us that Christ will enter into companionship, friendship, and intimacy with anyone who responds to His voice.

Also notice the word "with" in Revelation 3:20. It appears twice and is the Greek word *met' emou*, which is from the word *meta.* It depicts *companionship or close association.* It carries the idea of *doing something in conjunction with someone else; partnership.* Isn't it interesting that nowhere in this passage does Jesus penalize or punish the church of Laodicea for putting Him outside. Not once did He say, "I'm going to make you pay for the wrong you did before I sit down with you." On the contrary, His focus was on the restoration of relationship. The same holds true for you and every other child of God. What He cares about most is reconnecting with the people He loves.

You Are Called To Be an Overcomer!

Jesus went on to make a promise to the church of Laodicea — and to all believers of all generations. He said, "To him that overcometh will I grant to sit with me in my throne, even as I also overcame, and am set down with my Father in his throne" (Revelation 3:21). In the original Greek text, it does not say, "To him that overcometh." It says, "The overcoming one will...." In Greek, it is *ho Nikon*, which literally means *the one who is perpetually overcoming.* The word *Nikon* is from the root *nikao*, which describes *an overcomer, conqueror, champion, victor, master, or an overwhelming, prevailing force.* When compounded to form *ho Nikon*, it can be translated as *more than conquerors, overwhelming conquerors, victors paramount, or enormous overcomers.* This word is so power-packed that one could translate it as *a phenomenal, walloping conquering force.*

Make no mistake — as a child of God, you are not called to overcome just once or only on Sundays. You are called by God to be *a perpetual over-comer.* Day after day, week after week, month after month, and year after year; you are called to be a phenomenal, walloping force. You are a *victor,* not a victim. God wants you to live your life as the champion He created you to be in Christ.

To those who perpetually overcome, Jesus said, "will I grant to sit with me in my throne…" (Revelation 3:21). The phrase "will I grant" is the Greek word *doso*, which is a future form of the Greek word *didomi*, meaning *"I give."* In this verse, however, it could mean *"I allow"* or *"I permit."* Jesus said, "I will allow or permit anyone who perpetually overcomes to sit with me."

The words "to sit" in Greek is the word *kathidzo*, which means *to sit; to sit down*. Anyone who responds to Christ in obedience will be invited immediately — without delay — to sit with Him in His throne. Again, the word "with" is important. Here, it is the Greek word *met' emou*, and it depicts *companionship or close association; doing something in conjunction with someone else; partnership*. The phrase "in my throne" literally means, *"in the throne of Me."*

What is interesting here is the word for "throne" is *thronos*, and it denotes *the seat or throne for the head of a country or nation*. A king was the uncontested highest power of his country, and there was no higher authority, no higher law, and no higher power than the king in his own realm. Because he was endued with unmatched power and authority, he sat enthroned above all others. Jesus is the King of kings, and yet He says, "If you are an overcomer, I permit you to sit with Me on My very throne." That is absolutely amazing!

Keep in mind, Jesus is the ultimate overcomer. What He is asking us to do, He Himself had to do. He reminds us of this in Revelation 3:21 when He said, "…even as I also overcame…." The words "even as I" in Greek are *hos kago*, which mean, *I also; me too*. And the word "overcame" is *enikesa*, which is the past tense of the word *nikao* — the word translated as "overcometh" at the beginning of this verse. Again, it describes *an overcomer, conqueror, champion, victor, master, or an overwhelming, prevailing force*; it is a word so power-packed that one could translate it as *a phenomenal, walloping conquering force*.

Friend, God's highest call for you in this life is that you be a victor, not a victim. You are wired to perpetually overcome. You have been given the dynamic power of the Holy Spirit to overcome emotional struggles, negative and fearful thought patterns, financial challenges, and paralyzing addictions. **Through the empowering strength of Jesus Christ, you can do all things!**

STUDY QUESTIONS

> Study to shew thyself approved unto God, a workman that needeth
> not to be ashamed, rightly dividing the word of truth.
> — 2 Timothy 2:15

1. This life is full of challenges. Yet in spite of the hardships and trials we face, we are *overcomers* and *more than conquerors* in Christ. Take a few moments to meditate on these promises and personalize them by adding your name. How do these verses encourage and strengthen your faith?
   - **Romans 8:31-39**
   - **2 Corinthians 2:14**
   - **1 John 4:4; 5:4,5**
   - **2 Corinthians 10:3,4**
   - **Luke 10:19; Colossians 2:15**
   - **Matthew 16:19; 18:18-20**

2. Jesus is the ultimate Overcomer. He overcame the power of sin, Satan, and the flesh and then defeated death, hell, and the grave. Take time to reflect on Hebrews 2:14-18 and 4:14-16. How do these passages about Christ's humanity encourage you to run to Him for strength when you're being tempted?

PRACTICAL APPLICATION

> But be ye doers of the word, and not hearers only,
> deceiving your own selves.
> — James 1:22

1. How do you see yourself — as a *victim* or a *victor*? To help you accurately determine your answer, what kinds of things do you often find yourself thinking and saying? Are they words of victory or a reflection of a victim mentality?

2. What do you think it looks like to *perpetually overcome* the attacks and temptations of the enemy? What choices do you make day-in and day-out that help you stay in a position of victory?

3. Which habits, hang-ups, or temptations have you feeling most discouraged and defeated? If you're feeling depleted, take time now to pray and ask the Holy Spirit to give you the wisdom and strength you need to fight another day. (*See* Isaiah 40:28-31; Psalm 18:29; Philippians 2:13; 4:13.)

TOPIC

What the Spirit Is Saying to the Church Today

SCRIPTURES

1. **Revelation 3:14-22** — And unto the angel of the church of the Laodiceans write; These things saith the Amen, the faithful and true witness, the beginning of the creation of God; I know thy works, that thou art neither cold nor hot: I would thou wert cold or hot. So then because thou art lukewarm, and neither cold nor hot, I will spue thee out of my mouth. Because thou sayest, I am rich, and increased with goods, and have need of nothing; and knowest not that thou art wretched, and miserable, and poor, and blind, and naked: I counsel thee to buy of me gold tried in the fire, that thou mayest be rich; and white raiment, that thou mayest be clothed, and that the shame of thy nakedness do not appear; and anoint thine eyes with eyesalve, that thou mayest see. [I] as many as [if] I love, I rebuke and [I] chasten: be zealous therefore, and repent. Behold, I stand at the door, and knock: if any man hear my voice, and open the door, I will come in to him, and will sup with him, and he with me. To him that overcometh will I grant to sit with me in my throne, even as I also overcame, and am set down with my Father in his throne. He that hath an ear, let him hear what the Spirit saith unto the churches.

GREEK WORDS

1. "to him that overcometh" — ὁ νικῶν (*ho nikon*): the words ὁ νικῶν (*ho nikon*), literally, the one who is perpetually overcoming; the root

word **νικάω** (*nikao*) describes an overcomer, conqueror, champion, victor, master, or an overwhelming, prevailing force; when compounded, it can be translated as more than conquerors, overwhelming conquerors, victors paramount, or enormous overcomers; this word is so power-packed that one could translate it as a phenomenal, walloping conquering force

2. "will I grant" — **δώσω** (*doso*): a future form of the Greek word didomi, which means "I give," but in this verse could mean, "I allow or I permit"

3. "to sit" — **καθίζω** (*kathidzo*): to sit down; anyone who responds to Christ will be invited immediately to sit with Him in His throne; no delay, but immediately

4. "with" — **μετ' ἐμοῦ** (*met' emou*): depicts companionship or close association; to do something in conjunction with someone else; partnership

5. "even as I also" — **ὡς κἀγὼ** (*hos kago*): I also; me too

6. "am set down" — **καθίζω** (*kathidzo*): am presently seated

7. "with" — **μετ' ἐμοῦ** (*met' emou*): depicts companionship or close association; to do something in conjunction with someone else; partnership

8. "he that hath an ear" — **ὁ ἔχων οὖς** (*ho echo ous*): literally, the one having an ear; the word **ἔχω** (*exo*) means to have, hold, or possess; implies there are those who do not have an ear to hear; depicts anyone who possesses an ear to hear; one who can hear

9. "let him hear" — **ἀκούω** (*akouo*): hear or perceive; to comprehend by hearing; where we get the word acoustic

10. "what" — **τί** (*ti*): exactly what; precisely what; down to the most minute detail

SYNOPSIS

As we have seen throughout our study, the city of Laodicea was the wealthiest city in the Lycus Valley. It served as a banking center, a textile center, and a center for trade that regularly drew in thousands of people to buy and sell their goods. Epaphras, an associate of the apostle Paul, successfully established a church there — a church that was rich in material goods and finances and relatively free of resistance from the outside world. Sadly, by the end of the First Century, it entered a stage of spiritual decline. Their passion for Christ was neutralized, making them numb, calloused, and blind to their spiritual need.

After Jesus pointed out their desperate condition, He called them to repent and open the door of their lives so that He could enter once again. If they would hear and obey His words, He would immediately reconnect and reestablish an intimate relationship with them. This is the same message Christ is speaking to us today.

The emphasis of this lesson:

When Jesus said, "He that hath an ear, let him hear what the Spirit saith unto the churches" (Revelation 3:22), He wasn't just talking to the church of Laodicea. He was speaking to any believer — throughout all generations — who is listening and has an ear to hear what the Holy Spirit is saying to the Church.

A Final Review of Christ's Message to Laodicea

Jesus said,

> **And unto the angel of the church of the Laodiceans write;**
> **These things saith the Amen, the faithful and true witness, the beginning of the creation of God (Revelation 3:14).**

Remember, the word "angel" here refers to the *pastor* of the church. Your pastor is like an angel. He is God's appointed representative to speak on His behalf and help you grow and mature spiritually. Your pastor is always the first person Christ communicates to when He has something to say to your church.

This verse also tells us Jesus is the Faithful and True Witness who is trustworthy and reliable. He is the Originator, the Preeminent starting point, and the Source of all God's creation. He is also "the Amen." Again, this title has a definite article, which means Jesus is not just "an" amen — He is THE Amen. He is *the final word* on every subject, including every aspect of your life.

Christ went on to say,

> **I know thy works, that thou art neither cold nor hot: I would thou wert cold or hot. So then because thou art lukewarm, and**

neither cold nor hot, I will spue thee out of my mouth (Revelation 3:15,16).

In Jesus' eyes, being lukewarm is disgraceful. The Laodicean church had lost its spiritual fervency. It was no longer hot, like the healing waters of the city of Hierapolis to its north, and it was no longer freezing-cold, like the refreshing waters of the city of Colossae to the southeast. It had lost its redeeming value and become repugnant in the mouth of Jesus. Therefore, He was about to vomit the church of Laodicea out of His mouth.

Jesus had personally observed and knew (*oida*) the actions and activities of the Laodicean believers and had heard firsthand what they were saying about themselves. He said,

> **Because thou sayest, I am rich, and increased with goods, and have need of nothing; and knowest not that thou art wretched, and miserable, and poor, and blind, and naked (Revelation 3:17).**

We've seen that the words "I am" in Greek is the word *eimi*, which points to *self-reliance, self-focus, self-centeredness, and even self-absorption*. The Laodicean church had become the center of their world and were totally out of touch with the needs of others. They said they were "rich," which is the Greek word *Plousios*, describing *wealth so great it cannot be tabulated*. The fact that the word *Plousios* is capitalized here indicates that they believed they were *the richest of all the churches*.

Although in the natural, the church of Laodicea probably was the richest, spiritually it was the poorest. The Scripture says they claimed to be "increased with goods," which in Greek can be translated, *"I have made myself rich; I have resourced myself."* What's more, they also boasted to be in "need of nothing," which was the same as saying they had *absolutely no need of anything whatsoever*.

Motivated by love, Jesus set the record straight and revealed to the Laodiceans their true spiritual condition. He said, "...thou art wretched, and miserable, and poor, and blind, and naked" (Revelation 3:17). The meaning of the original Greek text here shows that this body of believers had become *the most calloused and miserable of all the churches*; they no longer had eyes to see their spiritual nakedness. Thus, they were to be greatly pitied.

Wanting desperately to lift the Laodiceans out of their misery, Jesus said,

I counsel thee to buy of me gold tried in the fire, that thou mayest be rich; and white raiment, that thou mayest be clothed, and that the shame of thy nakedness do not appear; and anoint thine eyes with eyesalve, that thou mayest see (Revelation 3:18).

The words "I counsel" in Greek is *sumbouleuo*, and it pictures *a joint counseling or a joint determination*. The word "thee" is the Greek word *soi*, which indicates that Jesus was *speaking directly to them, mincing no words*. Essentially, He got down on their level and candidly said, "Let's you and Me get together and make a wise decision about how to fix this issue and be determined to get you back on track."

Next, Jesus said, "…Buy of me gold tried in the fire, that thou mayest be rich…" (Revelation 3:18). The word "buy" is the Greek word *agoradzo*, which is from where we get the word *agora*, the term for a *marketplace*. Jesus' use of this word cut straight to the heart of the Laodiceans. Remember, they lived in a city with four massive marketplaces and about 4,500 shops set up along the roadway. If there was one thing they were extremely familiar with, it was shopping.

When Jesus said "buy of me," He was actually saying, "I am the marketplace you need. I am loaded with everything necessary to satisfy and fill the deficit you are experiencing." The tiny phrase "of me" is *par' emou* in Greek, and it means *from my side; available only at my side*. In other words, "If you'll come right alongside of Me and get as close to Me as you can," Jesus said, "you'll find what you need."

Specifically, Jesus said they were to buy "gold," which is the Greek word *chrusos*, the most valuable material that existed in the ancient world. It denotes that which is *rare and highly prized and of great significance*. This wasn't just any gold — it was the purest of gold "tried in the fire." The word "tried" is the Greek word *puro*, and it depicts *a purification and refining process*. Fire was used to purify, to burn rubbish, and to empower machinery. Symbolically, Christ was offering His holy fire to remove their calloused condition, purify their hearts, and empower them to get back on track. Buying gold — along with buying white raiment to clothe their spiritual nakedness — is what would make them truly rich!

Why did Jesus correct the church of Laodicea? It is the same reason He corrects any church or believer. He said,

As many as I *love*, I rebuke and chasten: be zealous therefore, and repent (Revelation 3:19).

Because Jesus genuinely loves us, He is going to expose our errors and convict us. He will then convince us of a new way of thinking and a new way of seeing things, all the while teaching us and training us with strict discipline to enable us to reach our full potential.

Where was Jesus and what was He doing when He said all these things to the Laodiceans? He answers this question in the next verse:

Behold, I stand at the door, and knock: if any man hear my voice, and open the door, I will come in to him, and will sup with him, and he with me (Revelation 3:20).

Jesus was *outside* of the church. When He said "Behold" — the Greek word *idou* — it was the equivalent of Him saying, "I am *shocked* with *wonder* and *amazement* at where I am. This is My Church, and I've been pushed out of it."

He continued, "I stand at the door and knock…." The words "I stand" is the Greek word *histemi*, meaning *I stand* or *I stand by*. The word "at" indicates *right there, right now*. Jesus was fully focused on regaining entrance into the church. Hence, He was right at "the door." The word "door" is the Greek word *thura*, and it describes *a large, solid door that is tightly sealed with a bolt that is slid through rings attached to the door and the frame*. When such doors were opened, it provided access that was normally restricted; hence, it denotes *an opportunity*.

Jesus earnestly awaited an *opportunity* to reenter the church of Laodicea. So He stood at the door and *knocked*. The word "knock" is the Greek word *krouo*, which describes *nonstop pounding*. The tense of this word means *to incessantly beat on a door, imploring one open the door by nonstop knocking and pounding*.

Then Jesus said, "…If any man hear my voice…." The word "if" indicates an invitation or offer. The phrase "any man" is the Greek word *tis*, meaning *anyone* — *any man or any woman*. The offer is to *anyone* who hears Jesus' "voice." The word "voice" in Greek is *phone*, and it describes *the sounds of words*. This is important as it tells us how Jesus "knocks." He doesn't actually pound on our hearts with His fist. He uses His *words*. Again and again and again, He speaks to us with words of correction, direction, caution, and warning. *His words are His knocking.*

To anyone who hears Jesus' voice and opens the door, He said, "…I will come in to him, and will sup with him, and he with me." The phrase "I will come" in Greek is *eiserchomai*, and it means *to immediately enter or quickly come right into*. The word "sup" is the Greek word *deipneo*, which describes *a late afternoon or early evening dinner that was reserved only for the closest of companions and friends*. The use of this word tells us that Christ will enter into companionship, friendship, and intimacy with anyone who responds to His voice.

> **To him that overcometh will I grant to sit with me in my throne, even as I also overcame, and am set down with my Father in his throne (Revelation 3:21).**

In our last lesson, we learned that the phrase "to him that overcometh" is *ho nikon* in Greek, which literally means *the one who is perpetually overcoming*. It is from the root word *nikao*, which describes *an overcomer, conqueror, champion, victor, master, or an overwhelming, prevailing force*. The word *ho nikon* is so power-packed that one could translate it as *a phenomenal, walloping conquering force*. The implication here is that there will always be something to overcome. But since Christ has overcome the world (*see* John 16:33), we too are overcomers in Him.

To all who perpetually overcome, Jesus said "…will I grant to sit with me in my throne, even as I also overcame…" (Revelation 3:21). The phrase "will I grant" is the Greek word *doso*, a future form of the word *didomi*, which means "I give." In this verse it means, "I allow or I permit." Hence, Jesus will give permission for overcomers "to sit" in His throne. In Greek, the words "to sit" is *kathidzo*, and it means *anyone who responds to Christ will be invited immediately to sit with Him in His throne without delay*. Even the word "with" is significant. It is the Greek word *met' emou*, and it depicts *companionship or close association; to do something in conjunction with someone else; partnership*.

It's important to note that Jesus said, "…even as I also overcame…." In Greek, "even as I also" means *I also; me too*. And the word "overcame" is *enikesa*, which is the past tense of the word *nikao* — the word translated "overcometh" at the beginning of the verse. Again, it describes *an overcomer, conqueror, champion, victor, master, or an overwhelming, prevailing force*. Think about it. Jesus — who is God in the flesh — already did what

He is asking us to do. And when He overcame, He was seated — and is still presently seated — with the Father on His throne. He is extending the same invitation to you when you overcome.

Jesus concluded His message to the church of Laodicea in the same way He concluded His message to each of the other six churches He addressed in Revelation 2 and 3. He said,

> **He that hath an ear, let him hear what the Spirit saith unto the churches (Revelation 3:22).**

The phrase "He that hath an ear" is a translation of the Greek words *ho echo ous*, and it literally means *the one having an ear*. The word *echo* means *to have, hold, or possess*. It implies there are those who do *not* have an ear to hear. Moreover, it depicts *anyone who possesses an ear to hear; one who can hear*.

This brings us to the phrase "let him hear," which is from the Greek word *akouo*, meaning *to hear or perceive; to comprehend by hearing*. It is from where we get the word *acoustic*. The word "what" is the Greek word *ti*, which means *exactly what; precisely what; down to the most minute detail*.

Thus, when Jesus said, "He that hath an ear, let him hear what the Spirit saith unto the churches" (Revelation 3:22), He was literally saying, "Anyone having an ear to hear, let him hear, perceive, and comprehend down to the most minute detail what the Holy Spirit is saying to the Church — which is all churches made up of all believers of all generations.

STUDY QUESTIONS

> Study to shew thyself approved unto God, a workman that needeth
> not to be ashamed, rightly dividing the word of truth.
> — 2 Timothy 2:15

1. Does it seem like God is silent in your life? What is the last thing you remember the Holy Spirit spoke to you? Did He ask you to do something specific? Were you obedient to what He asked?

2. Sometimes disobedience keeps us from hearing God's voice — it separates us from the intimacy He longs for. Carefully consider what He says in Acts 28:27; Ezekiel 12:2; First Samuel 12:15; 15:22; and Isaiah 59:1,2. Is God showing you any areas of your life where you haven't yet followed His instructions? Take time now to repent and

receive His mercy, forgiveness, and the grace to do what He's asked you to do.

3. According to John 14:23; 15:10; Matthew 7:24,25; James 1:25; Exodus 19:5; and First Kings 3:14, what are some of the blessings of *hearing* and *obeying* the voice of God?

PRACTICAL APPLICATION

But be ye doers of the word, and not hearers only,
deceiving your own selves.
— James 1:22

1. As you come to the end of this ten-lesson study on Christ's message to the church of Laodicea, what is your greatest takeaway? What truth from Scripture has the Holy Spirit really brought to life for you? In what ways has He shown you that you are like the church of Laodicea?

2. Now that you have heard some of the history concerning Laodicea, including its vast wealth and water problems, how might you share the importance of what Christ said to the church of Laodicea with a friend?

3. The phrase "He who has an ear" means *the one having an ear — one who has, holds, and possesses an ear to hear.* It implies there are those who do *not* have an ear to hear. Are you hearing the voice of Jesus? Take a moment to pray; "Lord, please give me ears to hear what You are saying, eyes to see where and how You are working, and a heart that promptly obeys what You are asking me to do (*see* Proverbs 20:12). Thank You for Your patience and love. In Jesus' name, Amen!"

Notes

Notes

Notes

Notes

_____

_____

_____

_____

_____

_____

_____

_____

_____

_____

_____

_____

_____

_____

_____

_____

_____

_____

_____

_____

_____

_____

_____

_____

_____

_____

_____

_____

www.ingramcontent.com/pod-product-compliance
Lightning Source LLC
Chambersburg PA
CBHW060402050426
42449CB00009B/1867